Eternal Consciousness:
Exploration of Infinite Perception

by Michael Townsand

RONIN
Berkeley, CA

Eternal Consciousness:
Exploration of Infinite Perception

by Michael Townsand

Eternal Consciousness: Exploration of Infinite Perception

Copyright 2018, 2021 by Michael Townsand
ISBN PBook: 9781579512903; ISBN EBook: 9781579512910

Published by
Ronin Publishing, Inc.
PO Box 3436
Oakland CA 94609
www.roninpub.com

Production:

    Cover Design: Brian Groppe
    Book Design: Beverly A. Potter
    Photos: Shutterstock

Library of Congress Card Number: -------
Manufactured in the United States by Lightning Source.
Distributed to the book trade by PGW/Ingram.

Acknowledgements

Dedicated to my dad John Townsand, who showed me firsthand that it really never ends.

William Leonard Pickard, for wise suggestions and kind encouragement early in the writing process.

The unseen hands that put obvious clues before me when I became lost, and the unseen spirit that encouraged me when I became doubtful.

My beloved wife Natasha and daughter Katie for their interest and support.

Tracy Wilborn for editing help.

My brothers Brian and John for interest and encouragement.

"What is matter without humankind, starlight without a flower? Can we apply our own values to the cosmos as a whole and uphold the poet's insight that one crowded hour of glorious life is worth an age without a name? Can we challenge the infinite with the intimate and emerge victorious? It is worth the try."

—M.J. Berrill
You and the Universe

Table of Contents

Table of Contents continued:

Preface

We live in an age not far removed from the religious and pseudo-religious schisms over the infinitude or finitude of the universe and, by logical extension, of the mind. Since the time of Epicurus and the Stoics in ancient Greece, and likely before, thinkers have argued and even died for the idea that the universe may be endless—and that all things happen over and over; all beings live infinite times and have endless possibilities.

There is great power in this debate, on one side for the individual, free-thinking mind; and on the other for those who wish to declare themselves authorities over the realities of the universe and existence. In every age there has been no shortage of the latter—and they have often tried to silence the former.

One of the more dramatic examples is the case of Giordano Bruno. Bruno was an Italian philosopher and scientist who was imprisoned for nearly eight years, tortured extensively and finally burned alive in a square in Rome called the Field of Flowers—

Thinkers have argued—and even died for the idea—that the universe may be endless and that all things happen over and over; all beings live infinite times and have endless possibilities.

simply because his ideas were considered heretical by the totalitarian religious establishment of his country.

One of Bruno's dangerous ideas, explained in his 1584 book, The Infinite Universe and its Worlds, was that there exists an infinite number of worlds and, within them, duplicates of all people and situations. Such thoughts were considered to be vestiges of the savage, ignorant pagan past. Bruno seemed to imply that all beings are eternal and thus divine. In the eyes of his judges, he was denying the special existential and spiritual status of saints and other traditional religious figures. He was thereby, supposedly, endangering the eternal souls of the common people. One cannot help but wonder whether the true reason for his persecution was that his ideas implied that all beings have equal value and standing in relation to the ultimate reality—and that the hierarchical advantages of the inquisitors were in peril.

That this idea might disturb and even enrage the authoritarian, absolutist 'thought police' of times much less free and tolerant than ours is obvious. What is not so obvious is that our modern, mainstream version of ultimate reality is still pseudo religious. Indeed, the finite view of the universe and consciousness has prevailed. Many think that this has little to no philosophical or logical basis. The infinite universe is still dangerous to those who have unnecessarily limited their starting assumptions and now struggle with the difficulties of an oversimplified and one-sided model of universal genesis and structure.

The heritage of thought on infinite worlds and existence handed down to us is extensive and rich, but it takes a lot of research to track down enough detail and depth to mold into a powerful theory to act as an alternative to the orthodox finite theory that is the view of the 'authorities' now. There seems to be more than a touch of the dogmatic in mainstream cosmology—and an underlying fear of being wrong appears to accompany it.

The heritage of thought on infinite worlds and existence handed down to us is extensive and rich.

Giordano Bruno's last words to his judges after being sentenced to be burned at the stake were, "Perhaps your fear in passing sentence upon me is greater than mine is in accepting it."

In his short story, *The Theologians*, Jorge Luis Borges uses a fictional story based on true events to examine the opposing philosophies and passions of both sides. He depicts a theologian who believes the universe and life are infinite being burned at the stake and yelling to his judges before he dies, "This has all happened and will happen again. You are not lighting a fire, you are lighting a labyrinth of flames. If all the fires I have been were gathered together here, they would not fit on earth and the angels would be blinded. I have said this many times."

Later in the story, the tables turn and the theologian who had had the man killed is himself sentenced to be burned alive for not believing in infinity. Unlike the believer in the infinite, right before his execution he "howls like an animal with his face in the dust" and has to be dragged to the stake. The implication is that in the end, his disbelief in infinite reality and his fear of death expose his true lack of faith.

In modern times, many feel torn between two seemingly contradictory ideologies: the empty reductionist science truism that all existence is 'just' atoms and molecules bouncing around randomly; and the apparently wishful thinking of eternal life, which has always had a metaphysical, non-scientific reputation. In fact, we need not be overawed by either science or spirituality, but only In modern times, many feel torn between two seemingly contradictory ideologies: the empty reductionist science truism that all existence is 'just' atoms and molecules bouncing around randomly; and the apparently wishful thinking of eternal life, which has always had a metaphysical, non-scientific reputation. In fact, we need not be overawed by either science or spirituality, but only to look at whether the ways they have been interpreted are based on solid foundations. Let us see if these two oversimplified caricatures are really so simple and so exclusive of each other after all.

1

Infinite Dreams

"…it all happened as it always does happen in dreams when you leap over space and time and the laws of nature and reason, and only pause at the points which are especially dear to your heart."

Fyodor Dostoevsky
The Dream of a Ridiculous Man

The prisoner was always very careful to avoid the small window of his cell. At night he could see a tiny patch of stars through it and, short of being released, he may have liked nothing better than to be able to get closer to that window to see more stars. The prisoner in question, Louis Auguste Blanqui, was a controversial and passionate character, very active in socialist politics. His ideas would eventually be used by both Marx and Mussolini. He was almost constantly in trouble with the government of his native France, which seemed to consider him a serious nuisance, and while he was serving this sentence the guards were ordered to shoot him if he got too close to the window.

Blanqui put together a grand hypothesis that all our lives go on forever at all times.

Blanqui's entanglement with infinity began in 1871. During one of several stints in prison, he wrote *Eternity by the Stars: An Astronomical Hypothesis*. Modern chemistry and astronomy were developing, and he used discoveries from these sciences to put together a grand hypothesis that all our lives go on forever at all times; life at a technical level is a pattern arrangement, and in our lives no event is final; all defeats and victories are endlessly recurring patterns.

Unfortunately Blanqui's book is often interpreted through a political lens, as a cosmological metaphor for socialist ideology; or as a consolation for the failures and frustrations of personally unrealized accomplishments – "Let us not forget that everything we could have been on this earth, we are it somewhere else." This politicization was nothing new. Political and religious convictions have complicated discussion of the ideas of infinity for much of history.

Georg Cantor, the mathematician famous for proving, in 1874, that there is an infinite number of infinities and that some are larger than others, died in a mental hospital. A common 'urban legend' about him is that overly intense, obsessive and drawn-out contemplation of infinity drove him insane. Could this legend have actually arisen from a projection of the fears of less rigorous, less brave minds—fears of the infinite and its ramifications? A smug spite for someone who dares to explore the wilds that they never could?

Today, Cantor's groundbreaking discoveries are widely used in mathematics, and are in fact the foundation of much of modern mathematics. However, his thoughtful, mystical potentials for ∞ have been replaced with a version that is a useful but simplified abstraction. The modern version of burning at the stake for infinite theorists has become a death of intellectual depth and passion on the icy stake of reductionism.

Amor Fati—Love of Fate

Philosopher extraordinaire Friedrich Nietzsche first wrote
about the 'Eternal Return' in 1882 in *The Joyful Wisdom*.
He tells us that the very possibility of eternal existence,
through the mechanisms of an infinite universe, is the
'thought of thoughts'—the most important question for
every thinking being; and, because of its unique weight for
the continued personal existence and ultimate fate of each
of us, it is the 'greatest burden'. Indeed, he thought that
we should want and love nothing more than to embrace
this possible fate and to see everything as a part of it: *amor
fati*—love of fate.

This idea was already an old one as the ancient
Egyptians, Greeks and Hebrews had all written of their
belief that everything exists forever and all events happen
again and again without end. Nietzsche brought the
Eternal Return back to western philosophy and science.

Interestingly, a popular belief about Nietzsche is
that he too was driven insane by his austere and lonely,
yet pioneering, philosophies. Much like Cantor, he took
infinity a lot more seriously than the average philosopher
or mathematician would. These two would have likely
appreciated a chance to help one another intellectually
with this 'greatest burden'. Cantor and Nietzsche both
wished to bring back the spiritual potentials of the infinite
that many of our human ancestors held as eternal truths.

An Idea Whose Time Had Come

In the 1870s and 1880s, it seemed to some that the infinite
and its implications for personal freedom and self-
actualization, was an idea whose time had come. These
were, after all, the decades when the groundwork for

Bruce Rolff

Entering Eternity

modern physics and chemistry was developed which led to many breathtaking discoveries and inventions – devices such as the telephone, light bulb, automobile, airplane and motion pictures. This was the age of the individual genius-inventor. An almost spiritual concept of endless creativity and endless potential through individual effort was coming to be.

Possibilities seemed to be infinite—an appearance supported by the wealth of scientific discoveries being made. Many thinkers also started to look back at ancient philosophies for evidence to support this belief in infinite possibilities—the central role of endless cycles in Indian and Egyptian religion, for instance.

Long before the small explosion of advanced mathematical and philosophical thinking on infinity of the late 19th century, another mathematician broke controversial ground. Safe in Britain, far from the reach of the Catholic Society of Jesuits—who had banned the idea of infinity in Italy and much of the continent—John Wallis was working on The Arithmetic of Infinitesimals, published in 1655. Wallis was one of the 'giants' of intellect upon whose shoulders Newton stood upon to invent the mathematical techniques of calculus. Similarly to the way Cantor's set theory was reinterpreted in a much simplified way, modern calculus replaces the concept of infinitely small actual quantities with the concept of limits at infinity that can be approached but never reached.

Wallis was one of the 'giants' of intellect upon whose shoulders Newton stood upon to invent the mathematical techniques of calculus.

Wallis lived in a time when his life could have been in danger if the Church had captured him. A physically safer time would have been the 1930s, when Jesuit priest Lemaitre supposedly 'discovered the beginning of the universe' with his idea of the 'primeval atom'—the Big Bang or Expanding Universe theory as it is now called. The connection of the Jesuit Society to conspiracy theories is often mocked, and sometimes rightly so; but how convenient is it that in this case one of them purportedly figured out exactly how the universe came about?

2

Eternal Consciousness
A Theory

Infinity and eternity were common ideas long before modern cosmological theories. The repeated return to those concepts is not a coincicdence or some kind of mass delusion. Rather, it strongly indicates that our ancestors had critical insights and longings.

Focusing on the experience of individual consciousness in its cosmological aspects, a theory— rooted in physical, individual, biological sentience—is offered in the following pages to help explain the existence and mechanisms of consciousness at pattern levels both smaller and larger than the observable universe. Aspects of it, including many of the foundational starting ideas, are ancient in origin; and many of the ideas were

Infinity and eternity were common ideas long before modern cosmological theories.

discovered independently in many different world cultures, since they are common intuitions.

Possibly the most scientific example comes from the ancient techniques of mental self-control developed in India over many centuries. Mishra's famous book *Fundamentals of Yoga* contains a passage that sums this up about as well as possible in just a few sentences:

In all organic beings, there dwells a marvelous secret power of freeing every being, of withdrawing the Self from material life, and of discovering the eternal in every being in the form of unchangeability. This experience of samadhi shows the seeker for the first time what real existence is. This occurs when one controls one's body, senses and mind, forgets them fully and identifies one's Self with the supreme Self. At this stage the seeker annihilates time and space and is no longer in time, but time and eternity are within. Anybody and everybody can feel it when ready. It gives the greatest enjoyment and immortality, and it requires the greatest sacrifice of materialism and mortality.

Cosmology

Cosmology is the study of the large-scale structure and behavior of the universe. This is the modern intellectual territory of astrophysicists, and sentience is irrelevant to the existence of astronomical bodies and processes. Cosmogeny is a subset of cosmology—specifically, the study of the origin of the universe. Cosmogeny, we will see, is dependent on sentience. Mainstream cosmogeny looks for an absolute beginning and end to the universe, but in our infinite, eternal universe there can be no absolute cosmogeny. There is no beginning or end in a pure physics sense.

Cosmogeny for purposes in this book indicates the creation of a perceptual world by a consciousness; and for a consciousness, unlike for the universe as a whole, there can be beginnings and ends. Cosmogeny is the study of how the cosmos is generated, and a unique cosmos is generated for every individual being by the perceptual activities and limitations of their biological structure—nervous system.

So, of course, the 'universally encompassing' cosmogeny of the mainstream is constrained by the limitations of the human nervous system. It follows that concepts of the universe made by any limited being are themselves limited. Any claims of an absolute structure or fate are dubious. The mysteries of the universe are equally accessible to those without advanced and specialized mathematics and physics knowledge.

Biocosmogenic theory offers mechanisms by which every individual consciousness eternally explores its infinite potential. This may sound New Age, but we will use mathematics and scientific principles to establish a likely path to this. The universe is infinite in many ways, in an infinite number of ways!

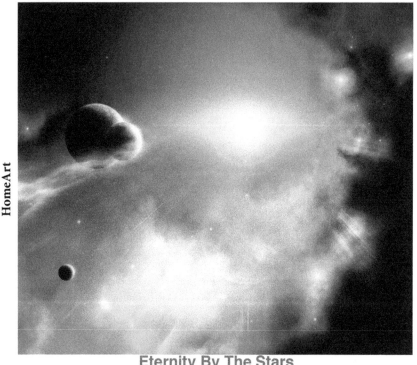

HomeArt

Eternity By The Stars

There are endless structural permutations that the components of the universe can and do take; endless levels of novelty created by the phenomenon of quantum size relativity in a realm of infinite matter and energy; endless nesting of realities, touching upon one another at every point of relative time. Eternal existence, adventure and peace are there for every consciousness. Of course, there is a lot of suffering in people's lives, and there are some who cannot see why they would want their individual life to be eternal; but the true self that has eternal peace exists just under the thin veneer of our everyday experiences and personalities.

Individual freedom, and an assurance from within our own being that 'all of this' means something and is going somewhere, is what we all really care about at the deepest level, and this theory provides possibilities for that as well. Giants of science, philosophy and spirituality, as well as countless unknown people through the ages, helped build the timeless intuitions and insights expressed here into their cultures so they could be handed down to us.

Many hope that science can be a tool to build a better world, though self-discovery. But can the ancient existential and spiritual questions of humanity be answered by science? Not completely; but it cannot hurt to use science to shine a new type of light on these questions. No theory, no matter how deep and detailed, can replace obligatory personal experience of the universe. The reality of existence begins with the personal. It depends upon individual consciousness. The type of finite-based science that looks at reality look from the outside stops at this threshold.

In building a theory of eternal individual consciousness —'life after death' is a dramatic way to say it—it is necessary to provide a physical cosmology to work out of. It is not a 'theory of everything'. Rather, it is a holistic cosmogenic theory derrived from merging physical cosmology with biology, as well as other sciences, to offer new insights and hope for what the existence of the individual may mean and be worth in the infinite universe.

3

Cosmology

Cosmogenesis is used here to mean creation of a personal reality from fundamental physical and associated neurological processes. Consider it one possible set of conceptual tools to help expansion beyond mainstream cosmology.

Modern cosmology attempts to explain the origin and deepest mechanisms of the universe from a finite and linear point of view. Things are reduced to particles and waves; and the universe is assumed, implicitly or explicitly, to be finite. These two assumptions are proper for the study of observable and finite physical objects, systems and processes. They have worked well to explain the non-conscious universe, in a similar way to how the assumptions of both earth-centric and Newtonian physics worked well until they reached their limits.

The modern cosmological approach is reductionist: it reduces complex systems to their simplest findable components. In this approach, the limits of our finite perceptions and concepts are taken, for purposes of convenience, to be the end. This is of course problematic

and this type of approach can **When consciousness is**
be called anti-Copernican. **considered in physics, it is**
Copernicus was the **from an outside viewpoint**
astronomer who proved that **rather than being subject**
the earth is not the center **to the full effects of it.**
of the known universe (the
known universe, at that time, was basically the solar
system). Cosmology needs a truly universal Copernican
Principle, which puts the greatest rigor into maintaining
common-sense logic and parsimony.

When consciousness is considered in physics, it is
from an outside viewpoint—someone observing a neural
impulse subject to the Heisenberg Uncertainty Principle
rather than being subject to the full effects of it. The infinite
extent and eternal complexity of the universe, however,
make this observational, scientific/technical paradigm
irrelevant for these largest questions of consciousness.

Resistance

The mainstream resistance to considering alternatives to
the standard cosmology seems to come from two things.
One is that the deeply ingrained mainstream approach
to scientific problems comes from an objective of control
over natural phenomena and resources for economic and
political goals; and the strategies used are communal
extensions of basic evolutionary struggle by individual
biological organisms. This is fine and necessary when the
goal is to help people—medical research, bioremediation
and so on—and to make a living; but, in basic research,
these motivations cannot be conducive to unprofitable
scientific pursuits such as individual cosmogeny, no matter
how legitimate and personally enriching they may be.

The second reason alternative theories, based on the ∞ and eternity of both the universe and the consciousness it contains, are hard to accept is simply how unusually subtle and difficult to grasp the full implications of the mechanisms of ∞ are. There is a consequent association with mysticism and religion that makes people turn away.

Scientific research often does start from pure, open wonder of reality and an honest thirst for knowledge. This happens at the level of the individual and the small, informal group level. However, after this free, adventurous phase, it goes into a social phase driven by evolutionary instincts for personal and group survival. Obviously, when we are considering the infinite universe and the individual's eternal existence within it, business as usual is out of the question.

Like others, such as Nietzsche and Cantor, I am going to try to extend science into the 'spiritual' field to help people of a more religious leaning to understand those with a more a scientific outlook. I am not claiming to give an authoritative account of reality; I just want to offer **The true essence and feeling of life is** another vantage point from which to observe the universe, one that **fascination and fun.** can be combined with other views from other vantage points. Spiritual seekers may find something here that at least gives them a better understanding of those who approach ultimate questions from a scientific direction. In some small way, I hope to bridge some gaps between two categories of thought which all too often separate people needlessly.

The true essence and feeling of life is fascination and fun. A myriad of human experiences across recorded history, in many cultures, indicates that there is 'something out there' as a popular television show used to say. It is the realm known by names such as mysticism, metaphysics and religion. It is speculation on otherworldly or spooky phenomena, on unseen, 'unknowable' aspects of our experience. Religions and other spiritual philosophies are traditional attempts to explain and systematize our instinctual feelings of eternal existence and worth. They tend to touch on basic truths with an intuitive sense, but they lack the scientific basis and intellectual rigor to build a case that could stand up to objective examination.

Another Way

Do you remember when you were a kid and you felt and experienced infinite realities emanating from everything? Maybe you still are a kid, but sadly many people do not remember, or at least do not know, how to fit eternal freedom back into their lives. When evolutionary pressures take over our attentions, and we have to fend for ourselves and families as adults, many of us forget that we have the ability to perceive infinite realities free of fear and worry. Usually, when this is acknowledged by an adult, it is dismissed as a charming but useless residue of childhood imagination. Often, when we get the rare chance to clear our minds, only boredom or doubt remain. These are poisons of the mind that are the sad result of forgetting the immortality and eternal peace all of us possess, and which is guaranteed mathematically and scientifically by the ∞ of all things.

We all have a strong sense of our personal worth and we can feel that same worth in others.

We all have a strong sense of our personal worth and we can feel that same worth in others. We call the latter respect and compassion. History, art and literature

are filled with examples of the depths of feelings of self-
worth and compassion and they have an important role
as adjuncts to a science of the absolute—which will, by its
nature, always be incomplete, mystical and individual . We
have the beginnings in science of an explanation, however
incomplete, of how everyday human consciousnesses can be reconciled with this transcendence. We all have the same potential connection
to universal Being—meaning our own pattern existence
beyond the personal ego. Your existence is eternal. It is your
job and your amazing privilege to explore the ∞ of your
own existence.

Many who are interested in cosmology but are not physicists often feel in a bind.

Many of us who are interested in cosmology but are
not physicists often feel in a bind. We recognize the impressive power of physics to describe and explain many
physical phenomena. We also see that physicists, just
like everyone else, can get stuck in assumptions that
are not necessarily more legitimate than others. This
can become obvious when anyone admirably tries to
extend the knowledge and techniques of their specialty
to the biggest questions that face us. Some of the result-
ing cosmological theories are compelling, while some
are bizarrely contrived and limited. Ours will be a view
from the fractal background matrix of the spectrum of the
known universe—from subatomic physics to astronomy.

4

More Science Please

Cosmology is, of course, based on astrophysics and quantum physics; but chemistry and biology can and should be worked in to link consciousness to cosmology. These two sciences are what the physiological and psychological sciences of human perception and consciousness are based on.

Science has reached a level of knowledge of the physical, chemical and biological systems of our cosmos that will let us start building theories to explain phenomena once thought to be forever in the realm of faith and closed to science. Science does not explain everything, such as what happens to consciousness after death.

Chemistry, biology and other fields of science are not best seen as branches of physics at different levels of size and complexity. They are fields that the human perceptual mechanisms naturally separate into functional areas characterized by completely **Science does not explain everything.** different regimes of emergent properties. These regimes make each separate field a clean break from its precedent and antecedent fields, though each is made up of elements of the precedent field. Reductionist science is very limiting, yet we invite it to be the final arbiter of the ultimate realities of the universe, including our own existences.

Why Cosmology?

Why cosmology from the perspective of chemistry and biology? Biology considers questions at higher orders on the spectrum of emergent properties. 'Higher order' just refers to more apparent complexity—it is not a value judgment ascribing higher importance or superiority to it. The science of biology has developed conceptual frameworks that can be used to transcend the oversimplified particle/wave movement concepts of physics. It has pattern equivalence models and mechanisms including a basic mechanism of pattern retention—DNA; and functional pattern change—natural selection of mutations and genetic recombination. Several levels of complexity come from these mechanisms—conserved systems retained over billions of generations—organismal evolution; and consciousness effects on relativity by conscious choice of stimuli and higher thought.

Biology also shares with physics a first cause difficulty—a central theory of a complex ancient genesis process. In biology, this is the problem of the origin of life. It is interesting to compare this with the mainstream physics theories of the origin of the universe—the expanding universe—or 'Big Bang'—and multiverse theories.

Maybe most importantly, biology is the science that addresses the most intimate questions of our existence by explaining the higher-order physical and energetic mechanisms of our human structure, which produces the individual sentience of each and every one of us.

Chemistry is the most solidly defined and self-contained scientific field and will be our connecting link from physics to biology/consciousness. It provides the most useful basis for mechanisms of cosmology relevant to a

Bruce Rolff

Science and Spirituality Come Together

conscious being who is not only in the universe, but of it. When taken as a separate body of knowledge, chemistry—and especially biochemistry—will be our touchstone.

We now have actual micrographs of atoms and molecules. Molecular orbital theory and other basic chemical theories that were worked out long before the microscopic technology was developed are now visually confirmed. Benzene rings are of the same composition and pattern as Kekule drew them in the mid-19th century, and they look exactly like molecular orbital theory predicts. It is the same story with all the tens of thousands of other molecules of organic chemistry. This is almost unprecedented in science and it makes chemistry the key—the starting point on which to build a more holistic biocosmogeny.

In the 1670s, Van Leeuwenhoek's microscope had a similar effect in the field of biology, opening paths to eternal fractal realities with visual confirmation of the previously theorized, but highly controversial, concepts of cells and microorganisms. The visual confirmation of molecular structure, though, was much more rigorous. It is a classic scientific success story of observations at a particular perceptual level leading to robust theory about realities at a very different perceptual levelone impossible to see or even imagine being possible to see at the time—confirmed later to be exactly correct.

This connection of the invisible to the visible links perception to cognition in the most convincing—and amazing—manner. Chemistry is not best seen as a subfield of physics any more than it should be seen as a mere prelude to biology.

Chemistry, with its theoretical methods and results, provides the human-scale link between physics and biology, illustrating the central role of pattern-dependent connections between different emergent property levels in cosmogeny. It deals with conceptual entities—atoms and molecules—that mainstream science accepts as pattern equivalent entities. Physics also deals with pattern equivalent entities—e.g. neutrinos, quarks,

This connection of the invisible to the visible links perception to cognition in the most convincing manner.

photons and waveforms—but these are more fundamental and farther from the functions of life.

Atoms & Molecules

Atoms and molecules are recognized as the most useful and convenient units to consider as the fundamental building blocks of life. Cells are technically the fundamental unit of life, as articulated in Schwann's cell theory, but they are not pattern equivalent from our perceptual level—they are pattern similar. Slight differences and mutations make cells individuals from our level of perceptive resolution. This is because we have the technical ability to study their microscopic structures and genetic variances. Biology works for us as a category of knowledge in the perceptual realm of pattern similarity; chemistry in that of pattern equivalence; and physics in that of fundamental energy processes and changes, like Einstein's equation $E=mc^2$ energy equals mass times the speed of light squared.

Atomic and molecular theory, evolution, Newtonian, Einsteinian and quantum physics, as well as chaos science, among many others, are all good resources with which to build a cosmology—along with ages-old intuitional/spiritual insights that we can observe, personally

The human mind is throughout our existence, a highly advanced instrument observing the parts of the universe accessible to it.

validate within our own minds, and use as higher-order data about our universe. Observations usually thought of as subjective experience may in many cases be too complex to integrate as legitimate data using current methods.

The human mind has been, throughout our existence, a highly advanced instrument observing the parts of the universe accessible to it. Many striking clues and conclusions about the nature of the actual world these observations represent have come out of the human nervous instrument itself over the millennia. Many appear to be functions universal to the human mind. They can and should be considered for use as a data set that just may have the potential, when ordered and disciplined by the laws of science, to expand the modern view of the universe.

Certain modes and functions of the mind have been chosen by history as the only legitimate ways to examine **Physical laws ensure** scientific questions; but innovation **that individual and** and change are also mainstays of **collective existence** history and thought. This could be **are in perfect balance.** characterized as a quest to find the 'objective within the subjective'— to discover, define and study the universally objective connections of human consciousness to the infinite.

Physical laws ensure that individual and collective existence are in perfect balance. It is important, in the unfolding cosmogeny of the physical individual, to elucidate and cultivate this balance, but individual obligations to evolutionary needs make this necessarily difficult.

5

Science, Philosophy & Perception

What we observe is not nature itself, but nature exposed to our method of questioning.

-Werner Heisenberg

The conceptual starting points of modern cosmogeny are something very human—assumptions. They are significantly arbitrary. Other concepts could just as well be used as foundations for cosmogenies. The important thing is to have the broadest and most possibility-rich conceptual framework. This way we cut out as much provincial cultural and religious baggage as possible, and we keep our interpretations of the universe open to ideas gleaned from interdisciplinary syntheses. This is the most rigorously scientific approach we can take.

> The important thing is to have the broadest and most possibility-rich conceptual framework.

A Logical Beginning

A portion of modern cosmologists work from unconscious, socially-conditioned assumptions about the fundamental nature of reality, matter and energy. These assumptions are not necessarily incorrect, but they are unexamined.

Formal philosophy laid the ground-work which enabled science to begin and to flourish. Some seem to think that an understanding of over 2000 years of rigorous work by many great philosophers is irrelevant to modern cosmology, but they do not realize that their starting assumptions are just an informal form of philosophizing. Formal philosophy laid the groundwork which enabled science to begin and to flourish. Using basic observation and logic, it worked out the conceptual foundations that allowed science to find its foothold and climb from there to greater realities. Early philosophy extensively studied questions like, what makes an object an individual, separate from other matter? What is space? What does it mean to know something? Going back to bedrock issues like this is needed for science to continue its climb.

Powerful Tools

The academic disciplines of philosophy, history and psychology are powerful tools with which to dissect the conceptual artifacts of modern cosmology and begin to get back to a more solid basis for cosmogony and cosmology. In the language of scientific experimentation, we need basic controls on our own minds in the practice of scientific cosmogeny and cosmology; and controls on the intrusion of our social conditioning and personal biases into science. These are necessary to make sure our theories are based upon the most objective, universal concepts and principles available to the platform of the human nervous system. These controls are best constructed with thoughtful and balanced use of the philosophical, psychological and historical knowledge, and experience gained over millennia by our ancestors.

What we would call science was called 'natural philosophy' in the 17th, 18th and 19th centuries. The separation of pure science from philosophy is a fairly recent development, and it is really an unfortunate and arbitrary limitation. In science, big ideas like cosmologies inevitably become politicized. The tension between the camps is shown by Michael White when he writes of Giordano Bruno:

"Bruno believed we are in direct communication with the divine, we are all part of the infinite. But to his enemies, infinity simply diminished, universality demeaned; and more than anything, it was this clash of ideologies that rested at the heart of their mutual hatred."

Political Universe

Finite universe cosmologist George Gamow was one of the main early developers of the Big Bang and felt that infinite universe theories were either in danger of being used in the service of communist ideology or were disguised expressions of it—remember Blanqui from the first chapter?—so he had his own non-scientific reasons to be against them from the start. David Bohm was an early developer of infinite multiverse theory. He was indeed a communist, and his ideas were largely dismissed, in part because of the mainstream fear of the connection.

Gamow as much as admits that it is more logical that the universe is infinite in his book, *One Two Three... Infinity*. He offers a thought experiment showing that even if every atom in the known universe were a printing press working at the speed of atomic vibrations since the supposed beginning of the universe, this would not be enough to print every possible book in English that might ever be written. With our knowledge of differential infinities, we can imagine

Prometheus Bringing Fire

the work that would be added if we expand the printing to every possible book in every possible language. Gamow has unconsciously touched on the critical role of consciousness in producing infinity here.

It is interesting, from a psychological point of view, that Gamow had been one of the Manhattan Project scientists who helped develop the first atomic bomb, and that he compared the Big Bang to this.

On the other side, infinite universe theorist and top astronomer Fred Hoyle felt that the 'Big Bang' as he mockingly named it during a radio interview, was being pushed as a religious dogma with a scientific veneer. The mainstream, including NASA, now uses the term without irony. Unfortunately, Hoyle had other opinions about scientific matters that made him look foolish, like thinking that Darwinian evolution is impossible and that life on earth came from microbes on meteorites. This caused his legitimate disagreement with the Big Bang to be disregarded without much fair debate.

The expanding universe theory was first proposed by the astronomer, physicist and Jesuit priest Georges Lemaitre. He called the point from which everything that exists supposedly came from 'the primeval atom'. Many of his fellow cosmologists, including Einstein, found this idea dubious, but it eventually became the accepted cosmological model because of its convenience. The problem, of course, is that it extrapolates what we see through the limits of our instruments as the limits of all existence; and the definition of universe is constrained purposely for convenience.

In 1951, a show was put on in which Pope Pius XII publicly declared that the theory validated Catholic theology. Lemaitre played the good scientist and responded that his theory was neutral, allowing the Church, which saw the modern scientific notation on the wall, to save face for its past sins vis-à-vis science and at the same time claim authoritative scientific validity of its creation doctrine with its followers.

Fractal—chaos—science has shown the big picture of how all patterns of matter and energy behave. Finite processes exist within a background of infinite matter, energy and space. **Finiteness is a localized property within infinite existence.** Finiteness is a localized property within infinite existence. Why would the universality of pattern complexity and change stop at any given level? It is not out of the question, but is there any convincing evidence, or even any good philosophical reason, for the assumption that there is an absolute starting and stopping point?

$$\infty$$

6

Setting Limits is Limiting

Electrons, protons, quarks and photons are called 'fundamental particles' but is there any basis for this besides the limitations of instrumental observation? These particles and others are the subjects of the scientific field of quantum mechanics. Quantum mechanics is not some incomprehensible magic, it is just a theory of energy levels and transactions within and between independent physical objects.

Is it possible that everything astrophysicists see is just a part of a mega galaxy that is among trillions of the same kind, with all of it part of a higher, even more complex particle? Is it possible that this pattern goes on infinitely and to take these infinite particles and every other individual piece of matter in the universe as quanta? It is a possibility that is usually not taken seriously but, for some reason, other odder conjectures are. Let us look into why.

Cosmogony is not just a matter of physics.

Cosmogony is not just a matter of physics. It depends also on basic human tendencies expressed through cultural worldviews and historical trends. If we do not consciously choose the conceptual frameworks that we apply our physical discoveries to, the final product will end up randomly cobbled together and weak. The field of academic philosophy uses some of the most profound human experiences, combined with logic, to construct basic starting points of thought—mental models of the paths we use to approach scientific study. History gives us a way to look at the development of ideas and human societies. This helps us to recognize provincial versus universal trends in thought. Psychology tells us of our needs for emotional and intellectual security and power, as well as how we construct our worldviews to achieve these personal and collective social goals.

All of the arguments for the universe not being infinite should be re-examined by modern cosmologies since the attitude toward ∞ is varied and not always consistent within any given theory. ∞ being difficult to work with is no excuse and it is unacceptable to simply assume the universe is finite.

Ancestral Wisdom

Mystics, priests, philosophers and scientists, in that order, have conjectured for millennia about the nature of reality –the 'truth'. From an objective viewpoint, this has produced ideas that inspired some of the people some of the time on an individual level; however, it sometimes created division between groups who, for various reasons—economic, political or otherwise, have claimed their concepts of the world to be absolute and infallible realities.

The role of religions, as pre-scientific philosophical systems, often containing striking insights into reality and the human condition is interesting. Many spiritual thinkers have seen the general outlines of infinite consciousness but interpreted them in a way that missed the simple explanation that reunifies troublesome dualities—often instead pushing them into an untouchable realm of otherness. The lack of a physically-based unifying theory caused them to fall back on mystical explanations with little or no grounding in objective reality. Ironically, this is the way that much of modern cosmology operates as well, with its lack of solid definitions for basic terms—the worst case being 'universe'—and disagreement about basic concepts like what 'space' is. Many religions and spiritual traditions correctly maintain that the individual lives on after physical death, and that this existence is eternal. This is based on physical reality, but before the discoveries of modern science it was not possible to hypothesize about the physical mechanisms of eternal consciousness.

Our scientific theories are shaped and limited by the concepts we start with. The range of possible explanatory modes for a theory to be based upon can often be limited by everyday things like the history of how a language developed to label certain concepts.

The following comparison shows how words can be made to mean more than we usually think, or different things than the current socially agreed upon meaning.

Nothing vs ∞

These two categories seem to be opposites, but in a certain semantic sense they can be equivalent. The word 'nothing' literally means 'no thing'. If we cannot mentally package an object, a pattern or process of nature into a symbol system—words, diagrams, illustrations or mathematical equations—t is 'not a thing'. If something does not fit into our symbol systems and our philosophical assumptions, it is not perceptually differentiated and assigned thingness.

Thingness and nothingness are very flexible concepts used for the convenience of the human mind, but the boundaries are not clear-cut. In a way 'nothing' can have existence if you think of it in literal terms as the opposite of matter and energy. In a similar way, the totality of existence that we cannot sense is assigned into the category of 'unknown'. This unknown 'no thingness' is verbalized a single thing, but it is actually an endless number of infinite sets of things. Some people would think this ∞ is 'no thing', that it does not exist because we will never directly sense it, even though logic and pattern science point to the universe being infinite.

The cosmological disagreements about the words 'space' and 'universe', what they are and what they do, come from a similar flexibility of interpretation of the possible meanings and use of words.

What Is Knowing?

If we take the word consciousness apart, we get two Latin terms—'con' which means 'with' and 'scier', which means 'to know'. Therefore, consciousness is literally the thing a living being knows things with. It is the biological mechanism that creates the process which filters and arranges outside sense impressions into forms (in-formation) that make the being do what it needs to survive and reproduce. All known consciousness comes from brains. From a neurologists point of view, consciousness is a complex pattern-forming property of the totality of chemical reactions and electrical impulses moving around the brain. This stark scientific explanation is only a simplified preliminary map to point the way on out exploration of infinite consciousness. We need other techniques to get deeper into the meaning of consciousness. The field of philosophy that looks at what it means to know is epistemology. However, from a simplified biological view, to 'know' is for a brain to make neural patterns that correspond to relevant outside stimuli.

7

Models of Reality

Our ideas of what science is, and our expectations of what it can accomplish, determine our scope of possibilities for ultimate answers of existence based on science. Mainstream cosmology wants a theory of everything and mostly insists, explicitly or implicitly that the universe be treated as finite, even when it is admitted that it may not be. David Deutsch in *The Fabric of Reality* writes:

> *"A reductionist thinks that science is about analyzing things into components. An instrumentalist thinks science is about predicting things. To either of them, the existence of high-level sciences is merely a matter of convenience. Complexity prevents us from using fundamental physics to make high-level predictions, so instead we guess what those predictions would be if we could make them –emergence gives us a chance of doing that successfully –and, supposedly, that is what the higher-level sciences are about. Thus to reductionists and instrumentalists, who disregard both the real structure and the real purpose of scientific knowledge, the base of the predictive hierarchy of physics is by definition the 'theory of everything'."*

Many biologists would love to find an unknown fundamental biological process, but we would not expect it to be able to explain the whole of biology in isolation. Even the discovery of DNA, its mechanisms and its functions didn't explain biology as a whole. We still need cell biology, zoology, botany, ecology, and so on, to give a more complete picture of the processes and patterns of life in the world. Cosmology is a high-level science and, like biology, it needs to be pursued in a similar holistic way. The finite expansion theory of cosmology is mostly limited to the usual physics. Mathematical ∞ combined with interdisciplinary pattern science offers a vastly richer palette of possibilities.

In science, you do not get very far without solid definitions, which are fundamental conceptual starting points. Shifting, vague definitions or, even worse, undefined terms, make meaningful theoretical work impossible. Commonly used and essential terms like 'universe', 'reality' and 'nature' have historically gone undefined, or at least poorly and inconsistently defined. Think about this—how could chemistry function as a science if 'atom', 'molecule' and 'energy' were undefined or poorly defined? What would biology be if 'cell' and 'organism' were fuzzily defined? Or if different researchers had different definitions?

Definition Issue

The definition issue is one of the main reasons for the difficulty in making useful interpretations and reaching significant consensus on the scope and possibilities in cosmology. Well-known physicist Sir Roger Penrose says, in regard to the differing behavior of molecules and supramolecular objects, "Something has got to go wrong with quantum mechanics somewhere, I regard this as a major problem that is going to require another revolution."

In science, you do not get very far without solid definitions, which are fundamental conceptual starting points.

What has gone wrong most likely involves basic misinterpretations of fundamental concepts like space, time and universe. To see how basic philosophy uses rigorous logic to define basic terms and could help in building the foundations of modern cosmogony, let us look at how a well-known ancient philosopher addressed the question of whether the universe is infinite or not.

The Logic of ∞

Many thinkers and religions of the ancient world held the universe to be infinite. Roman poet and philosopher Lucretius, a student of Greek philosopher Epicurus, in his epic book, *On the Nature of Things*, relates to us a compelling argument for the ∞ of the universe. He starts from the first principle of the duality of matter and void. These are the two basic categories of reality, the ultimate way to reduce everything we observe and experience into two opposing types. Lucretius first says that if there is a 'border' of the universe—if matter is finite—there is necessarily void outside of it and that this void is part of the universe as well.

He offers the thought experiment of a spear being thrown into the void. The spear can do one of only two things: stop, when it runs into a bigger piece of matter; or continue to fly endlessly through the void. The void is defined as the entity which gives place to matter. It is also known as 'space'. Lucretius wrote, "The result will be that an end can nowhere be fixed, and the room given for flight will still prolong the power of flight." He introduces to us the idea that space never ends and always has the potential to contain matter and energy. Lucretius grasped

If space extends infinitely, it is obviously possible for infinite matter to exist within it.

Space Energy and Particles

the truth behind Newton's 1st law: an object in motion
will remain in motion, unless a force acts upon it. And
over 2000 years ago, he correctly predicted the behavior
of an object in outer space. He defined cosmological terms
carefully—space' for example.

For us, essentially the spear represents the physical
possibility of infinite extension of the universe and of
sensory potential. Simple thought experiments like this
are still able to show us basic fundamentals that
should be used to construct cosmological theories.
If space extends infinitely, it is obviously possible for
infinite matter to exist within it. Indeed, it becomes
absurd to say that where we are in the universe
is the only spot with matter in it. It becomes anti-
Copernican. Once again, we must remind ourselves
that we are not the center of it all.

The important point in this for modern cosmology is

that Lucretius shows that there is no reason to assume that any universal 'border' of matter, including our modern 'border', defined as the edge of what we can sense through telescopes, is a legitimate cosmological assumption. It is common sense to conclude that there can always be more matter after a length of void, as we observe endless phenomena everyday based on the fact of matter separated by space. From basic logic, he informs us there are only three possibilities:

"Again, nature keeps the sum of things from setting any limit to itself since she compels body to be ended by void and void in turn by body, so that either she thus renders the universe infinite by alternation of the two, or else the one of the two, in which case the other does not bound it, with its single nature stretching nevertheless immeasurably.

Lucretius touches all the bases in his argument about the ∞ of the universe. It is a wonderful instance of impeccable reasoning beginning from universally observed first principles and expanding to explain specific cases. Compare this with modern cosmology, which mostly starts from highly technical observations

Lucretius touches all the bases in his argument about the ∞ of the universe.

of specific cases—astronomical objects and subatomic particles—which are then shoehorned into a framework of assumptions based on the idea of a finite universe. Lucretius' logic for three possible states makes obvious the contrived nature of the modern idea of a local collection of matter surrounded by infinite nothingness, which is supposedly not even space!

8

The Problem of Space

Modern cosmology can only insist on a finite universe and explain Lucretian logic away by saying that the space between stars and galaxies is somehow different from the void that would logically be outside of the known universe. Some cosmologists say that what we think of as empty space is not empty. They mean that even interstellar space, which looks empty through any type of astronomical instrument, has photons, atoms and electrons in it at extremely minute concentrations. Some imply that this means that space does not really exist.

This is, at best, a fascinating example of disregard of philosophical rigor. If you had an area of interstellar space 1 cubic meter in volume, containing only a single hydrogen atom exactly in the center, you can say this particularly defined space is not empty, but you can say that the space defined as a single cubic centimeter located 5 centimeters away from the atom is truly empty. Obviously, framing matters.

Some cosmologists say that what we think of as empty space is not empty.

In his spoof of cosmology, *Cosmicomics*, Italo Calvino points out:

> *"...if it was true that space with something inside is different from empty space because the matter causes a curving*

or a tautness which makes all the lines contained in space
curve or tauten, then the line each of us was following was
straight in the only way a straight line can be straight:
namely deformed to the extent that the limpid harmony
of the general void is deformed by the clutter of matter, in
other words, twisting all around this bump or pimple or
excrescence which is the universe in the midst of space."

The argument is also put forth that energy goes through
all of space, filling it, and so there is no such thing as
void. Evidence given for this is that from anywhere in
the universe, you will see
light. We see light from
billions of years ago, from
the farthest stars we see
through our telescopes.

We see light from billions of years ago, from the farthest stars we see through our telescopes.

Some cosmologists take this to mean that if the universe
were infinite, we would see infinite light around us. This
overlaps with Olber's Paradox, which is the idea that since
the night sky is not completely filled by infinite starlight,
the universe cannot be infinite.

Mandlebrot's Solution

A solution was given by Benoit Mandelbrot, who
discovered the first known fractal set, now known as the
Mandelbrot set. He maintained that fractal geometry could
explain Olber's Paradox in the infinite universe. Different
size-relative levels of reality at infinite scaling would make
an infinite universe even if we discovered matter to be
'finite' at our size pattern level—galactic clusters within
subatomic particles, for example.

The current definition of 'matter' as being made of
atoms and subatomic particles would then be limited and
only apply as a size-relative convenience. 'Matter' would

have to be redefined in a more comprehensive way. The overly simple assumption of Olber's Paradox that the sky would have to shine with infinite starlight is another anti-Copernican obstacle to a much more elegant and richer approach to cosmology. There is no sound reason to assume

Laouredin

Mandelbrot Sets

that we are in a situation to see all light in the universe. It is even possible to turn the paradox around and propose that the much touted 'cosmic background radiation' is what we

observe from ∞ instead of light, and that it is actually evidence for the infinite universe.

Lucretius even addresses what we now call entropy and the possibility of the 'Big Crunch'—the opposite of the Big Bang in modern cosmology. He concludes that if void were infinite and matter finite:

> *"Neither sea nor earth nor glittering quarters of heaven nor mortal kind... could hold their ground one brief passing hour; since forced asunder from its union, the store of matter would be dissolved and borne along the mighty void, or rather I should say, would never have combined to produce anything, since scattered abroad it could never have been brought together."*

Something From Nothing?

The ancient Greek school of philosophy called the Stoics came up with the first known naturalistic concept of physical energy exchange—entropy. They called it condensation and rarefaction, matter coming together or moving apart. In a very early approach to the conception of thermodynamic processes in the natural world, the Stoics assigned a dynamic role to fire, which is what they thought of as pure energy in all areas of natural phenomena—indeed, in the cosmos itself as a whole.

This is very possibly the philosophical root of the Big Bang/Crunch idea. However, whether the visible universe is expanding or contracting is only a provincial question that avoids the truly Copernican conclusion that the most logical and likely large-scale structure of the universe is represented by infinitely repeating and simultaneously, infinitely diverse fractal size relativity in both size directions. The particular properties of any given natural phenomenon at a single size level should not distract us from true universal structure and function.

Lucretius stresses that things do not come from nothing, defying the belief in the all-pervading power of the gods which was a hallmark of his time.

Early in his book, Lucretius stresses that things do not come from nothing, defying the belief in the all-pervading power of the gods which was a hallmark of his time. This principle is still valid today, defying the modern Big Bang belief in everything springing from nothing—or next to nothing. Occam's razor and the Copernican principle tell us that it is exceedingly unlikely that we are near the center of everything, or that there is even a center to speak of.

The Rejuvenation of Matter

The only logical way to rationalize a Big Bang/Big Crunch of a finite universe is to assume that everything we see is just a unit in a field of other similar units, analogous to an atom in a sea of other atoms. The idea that the universe is 'fine-tuned' for life to begin and evolve to a high complexity is a common one used by advocates of 'intelligent design', the insistence that an intelligence had to have designed the universe.

This is an attempt to justify denial of biological evolution in order to salvage religious dogmas of creation. It is also used by some mainstream cosmologists, which is odd and counterintuitive if they do not hypothesize an infinite universe. Logically, if there are infinite Big Bang units, the fact that ours has the perfect conditions for life is not so amazing—there are infinite chances for it to be so, and we are necessarily in one where it is! If one puts forth a finite universe, it is much less logical that one would just happen to be so nearly perfect for life by chance.

Lucretius stipulates the 'need' for infinite matter to refresh worn out matter—broken-down patterns—throughout the universe. This is often misinterpreted as creation of matter from nothing, but he means that infinite matter on all sides of all other matter is the only logical way for the universe to continually rejuvenate itself and continue. Lucretius is saying that an infinite amount of matter contains itself without the need for an actual, finite gravitational 'container'.

9

Entropy & Energy

The 'different space' mentioned earlier is one way finite theorists have tried to make a container for the universe. In physics, the principle of entropy says that matter with more energy gives its excess to less energetic neighbors. Finite cosmologists use this against the infinite universe, saying that eventually the entirety of existence would run out of energy; but in the infinite universe, as local energy runs out, energy flows back in from sections of the fractal dimension outside or inside the particular size level of matter in question.

Mandelbrot's fractal geometry defense of the ∞ of the universe covers the infinite availability of energy as well as the mechanism of trapping starlight. On the first point, different size-relative levels of reality can contribute energy to others. Think of the vast amount of energy released from the atomic level by a nuclear bomb. From a few **Think of the vast** pounds of metal atoms, more energy is **amount of energy** released in a few milliseconds than is **released from the** produced by thousands of tons of coal **atomic level by a** at molecular level. This is an effect so **nuclear bomb.** extreme and unexpected as to look like sorcery to most non-physicists. Even most physicists, before the theoretical development and the testing of atomic energy technology, would likely have found these amounts of energy nearly unbelievable.

You can see why many cosmologists would find the next possible levels of mass/energy phenomena within the pattern structures of ∞ mind-boggling and even deny them as impossible. The principle of entropy is not violated by ∞.

The Diversity of ∞

German mathematician Georg Cantor proved that there exists an ∞ of infinities. His most important contribution to mathematics was Set Theory, which deals with the mathematical ability to categorize all possible patterns into sets. Cantor called the totality of them, the set of all sets, Absolute ∞. He felt that this was not merely a mathematical abstraction, but that it reflected the real state of all matter, energy and space in the universe as well as every physically possible configuration of these components. During his lifetime, Cantor was aggressively attacked by some well-known mathematicians and philosophers. He was called a 'scientific charlatan' and set theory was labeled as 'nonsense' among many other insults. Such is the fear of ∞. Cantor can rest easy, though, because set theory is now the standard foundation of mathematics.

According to the *Stanford Encyclopedia of Philosophy*:

"Set theory is the mathematical theory of well-determined collections called sets, of objects that are called members, or elements, of the set. Pure set theory deals exclusively with sets, so the only sets under consideration are those whose members are also sets. The essence of set theory is the study of infinite sets, and therefore it can be defined as the mathematical theory of the actual — as opposed to potential — infinite."

The notion of set is so simple that it is usually introduced informally, and regarded as self-evident.

The notion of set is so simple that it is usually introduced informally, and regarded as self-evident. In set theory, however, as is usual in mathematics, sets are given axiomatically, so their existence and basic properties are postulated by the appropriate formal axioms. The axioms of set theory imply the existence of a set-theoretic universe so rich that all mathematical objects can be construed as sets. Thus, set theory has become the standard foundation for mathematics, as every mathematical object can be viewed as a set.

Both aspects of set theory, namely, as the mathematical science of the infinite, and as the foundation of mathematics, are of philosophical importance.

Set Theory and Infinity

One of the most important points of set theory for us is that a set can be infinite but not include everything –it is a matter of categorization, and there are different 'sizes' of infinite sets. For example, there exists an ∞ of whole numbers as well as an infinite amount of decimal numbers. The decimal point adds an additional dimension of infinity.

We can define a set as containing an ∞ of threes or of electrons. The set of threes, though infinite itself, is in fact infinitely smaller than the set defined as containing an infinite amount of every single whole number—infinite ones, infinite twos and so on.

The set of infinite electrons is infinitely smaller—in variety, not size—than the set of all possible fish species that could evolve in an infinite, eternal universe because 'electron' and 'three' as categories are self-limiting. They are specific identities, while the categories 'number' or 'fish' are not; because there are infinite possible variations within these categories. They are identity types, not specific identities. We can see how this is perception dependent. The resolution of our senses and our scope of knowledge determine what sense objects we assign to different sets. The philosophical basis for this was refined by Arthur Schopenhauer in his main work—*The World as Will and Representation* in 1818. Schopenhauer details how.

The 'size' of a set is immaterial—because it is relative; it is variety that makes the difference. Size is a relative property of finite relations that is meaningless in calculations of ∞. You see, since some infinite sets have infinitely more content in a variety sense than others, some infinite sets can be infinitely 'larger' than other infinite sets. This is hard to grasp and it was one of the most shocking and, to some, disturbing discoveries made by Cantor about the nature of ∞. His application of these findings to physical reality itself, and especially his extension of them into spiritual/religious beliefs, set many people against him.

> **The 'size' of a set is immaterial—because it is relative; it is variety that makes the difference.**

10

Timelessness & ∞

The infinite universe possesses an ∞ of static—
timeless—moments of existence, like snapshots
frozen in time. It also possesses an infinite number of
dynamic events—infinite time—like videos that contain
movement and change. These two categories exist always
and simultaneously. They 'come into existence' as separate
sets—experiences in our perception—when we focus on
one of them to the exclusion of the other and interpret
them as 'events' and 'moments'.

It is important to note that something exists—matter
and energy in patterns and movement trajectories—even
when we don't fix our perceptual
mechanisms on them. We are
not just imagining things that
are not there or creating reality
from nothing. That is why it is
specified that actual infinite sets
must contain only physically possible objects, concepts and
events. The set of infinite number threes, for example, is a
snapshot set, while the set of all possible movements and
thoughts of a particular person is a dynamic set.

We are not just imagining things that are not there or creating reality from nothing.

There are people who say the finite cannot contain the
infinite and that the two categories are mutually exclusive.
However, imagine a child playing in a huge field with

many tens of thousands of flowers scattered throughout. The child is playing a game of forging a path from flower to flower. An almost endless variety of paths is open to the child in this field of flowers—more than he or she could ever trace in a lifetime. Of course, since the number of flowers is finite, a fun-spoiling technician could come along and do some satellite imaging, have a computer count the flowers, trace every path within a few seconds and declare that 'we' understand every path possible through that particular pattern configuration—naturally, boring everyone almost to tears except themselves in the process.

If, however, we consider an infinite field of flowers, or an infinite set of finite fields where each field differs, the fun-killing technicians and their essentially empty symbolic calculations are held forever at bay. Actual infinite realities invalidate provincial symbolic limitations.

Infinite Sets, Infinite Possibilities

We continue our categorization by breaking down the static ∞ of timeless, frozen moments into an infinite number of sets, each of which contains, by conscious choice, one and only one timeless moment. These moments, of course, exist in their own infinite subsets. A moment becomes 'infinite' through the absolute attention of a consciousness.

Often, the absurdities that can be conjured up from infinite set theory, that may seem logically unavoidable, are cited as damning evidence against an infinite universe. There is an oft-quoted one about thousands of monkeys on typewriters eventually writing a Shakespeare play, given an infinite amount of time. Hypothetical situations like this are misleading. The

A moment becomes 'infinite' through the absolute attention of a consciousness.

presence of an infinity of imaginable permutations does not mean that everything imaginable does happen. It simply means that there are infinite possibilities. The impossible remains impossible. The monkeys would not write a play like a human does. It could eventually get done, but someone would have to go through all the random writings for years and splice together the correct words and chance combinations of words into the play. A sufficient pattern mechanism must act upon a set to form it in a certain way—in this case a human with sufficient editing skills.

Some cosmologists have used the term 'boundary at ∞ in an absolute sense. This is meaningless, as we know from our study of the basic properties of infinites and the existence of differential infinities. ∞ is not an object, a limit or a place. It is a property of the universe, creating a different set for each defined pattern unit it is used for. An infinite boundary would only exist in reference to its contents and does not bound other infinities.

The Nature of ∞

The most common mistake here is thinking of ∞ as a singular, absolute thing. The greater diversity of pattern sets making up higher-order infinities outstrips the infinite boundary of a more narrowly defined infinite set. There are also relative sizes—or better scopes—of ∞ categories of the same type. For example, the infinite set defined as all jelly bean flavors possible in the universe is larger than the infinite set which includes only cherry jelly beans.

If one thinks of ∞ in terms of numbers, all infinite sets are the same—a set of symbols representing objects endlessly increasing in digits, or fractions with the denominator getting endlessly larger. Who thinks of one type of thing as being the same as a group of endless types of things though?

The differentiation of infinities comes from conscious perception of diversity and novelty in a set. It is a discrimination of type categories. In this example, 'cherry jelly bean' is a defined category type. However, we could differentiate between an infinite number of individual cherry jelly beans if we wanted to—and if we had the perceptual tools to find and define more and more detailed atomic and molecular differences between individual cherry jelly beans.

The differentiation of infinities comes from conscious perception of diversity and

The Directionality of ∞

Another important property of infinite sets is that they can have directionality. Think of one of the simplest of infinite sets: 1 to ∞. This uni-directional set begins at an exact point—1—and never ends. The choice of limits once again defines this function. We can define a set going in the opposite direction: 1 to 0. This is an infinite set, but is often thought of inaccurately as finite because it approaches zero. To represent it, we can choose a finite number of decimal places: 0.999999,0.999998,0.999997 and so on, and we eventually reach zero.

However, choosing a finite number of decimal places in this way results in the set becoming finite. The point is that the number of possible decimal places is infinite—the number one can be subdivided infinitely, which means that the set of all numbers from 1 to 0 is infinite even though it approaches zero.

Choosing a finite number of decimal places in this way results in the set becoming finite.

∞, One, and Zero

A better name for zero may be negative ∞—it is infinite relative to the number one. Any number of digits can be put after the decimal point, just like any number of digits can be imagined in front of the decimal in the set 1 to ∞. When we put these sets together, we get a two directional set that increases in size in one direction and decreases in the other. Another mathematical name for the number one is 'unity', and this combined set unifies positive and negative infinites at the meeting point of 'one'. Unity represents the perspective of a conscious observer in the concept of size relativity' of actual universal objects in both size directions. This is something that we will cover later.

Another interesting point is that the number 1, representing the observer, is seen to be an ∞ relative to zero, since it can be infinitely subdivided as it approaches zero. However, the fixed value in these relations, either one or zero, is finite relative to the ∞ it approaches. Think about this in terms of the relativity of infinites concerned with separation into type categories and you will start to feel the mathematics of Mandelbrot's fractal geometry justification for an infinite universe.

Mathematics has had the concept of an ∞ of infinites. Let us not worry about 'number'. Instead focus on the variety of infinite sets of every situation. Think of ∞ as a very flexible tool used to define endless varieties of pattern mechanisms. These pattern mechanisms are formed by perceptual sorting of real objects and processes into sets. It is easy to stumble on the concept of ∞ and dismiss it as a simple mathematical abstraction. If we accept the intellectual laziness, we lose the essential ingredient of a mature cosmology. ∞ is not just an endless number, or even a vague, formless endlessness of experience.

11

The Absolute & The Relative

Perceptible differences are limited by the structures and tolerances of our senses and instruments. The two sub-branches are categories differentiated by conscious focus. Absolute ∞ is the only independently existing entity.

Sub-Branches of Absolute ∞

∞ of Static Diversity—the infinite existence of all physically possible states and their combinations: infinite snapshots—matter.

∞ of Dynamic Variation—the infinite existence of all processes and their combinations: infinite movement in all possible configurations of matter—energy

A consciousness is a type of quantum object which delimits and orders finite portions of that absolute ∞. This is the result of the limitation of finite individual perception. The sense we make of anything in our world is by restricting our perception to certain subsets of patterns. That is how the animal mind works to survive and reproduce. The human mind constructs a life on the foundation of this perceptual imperative. The nervous system that does this has evolved, as a result of survival and reproductive pressures, because it was physically possible on this planet.

Since we reached a certain evolutionary threshold, the individual human has possessed the capacity to **Time is the way** choose which perceptual pattern **we measure** regimes to focus on. We are not nearly **relative change** as constrained as most animals to **in matter.** instinctual reactions to stimuli. We understand perceptual stimuli as arbitrary to a certain extent. We can choose to see a sense object as a concrete physical existence, or as an abstraction. Imagine infinite clouds in an infinite sky. If one had an eternity, one could choose to see any combination of images and patterns of images, at any level of complexity, linked together in any combination.

A Return to Reason

Time and space, in Einstein's general relativity theory, are welded together into a thing called spacetime, which is considered real enough to form geometrical structures. Time is treated as a physical entity in spacetime, not just the standardized human measure of change. Many people are either confused or dazzled by relativity theory, but the geometrical structures supposedly formed by spacetime are simply a useful shorthand method for physics.

The common way one hears it is that time is a property of space, forming Einstein's spacetime; but this is looking at it in reverse, without considering matter. Space is necessary for movement of matter and energy to occur; but without matter or energy, change does not occur. Time is our measurement of our perception of relative change in matter and energy. Without a conscious perceiver, change occurs, but time does not. Calling time a property of space is not mystical or confusing; it is just a way to say that space gives place to matter and energy, and that matter and energy change—just like Lucretius said thousands of years ago. It eliminates the matter/space duality from the equation, conveniently simplifying many calculations.

Space, Time, and the Void

To get closer to reality, though, we may need to discard spacetime and go back to fundamentals. Our instincts are largely correct about the basics of space and time. Space, void, nothing and emptiness are the sam—simply the lack of matter and energy within a defined area relative to observed matter and energy. This concept is the essential counterpoint to matter and energy. It is the property of giving matter and energy measurable volume and velocity as well as the ability to change relative physical location.

Time is the way we measure relative change in matter. Movement relative to other objects and within objects is essential for change. That is why thinking of spacetime as a real thing, with separate existence, is suspect. Linking time to space through the property of relativistic change in matter is a way to look at the universe in the negative, like the negative of a photo. This may be useful for some theoretical details, but spacetime is really just a convenient concept for physic—a different perspective from which to look at reality.

Time is the way we measure relative change in matter.

Author Italo Calvino, in *Cosmicomics*, continues:

"...we should always bear in mind how space breaks up around every cherry tree and every leaf of every bough that moves in the wind, and at every indentation of the edge

*of every leaf, and also it forms along every vein of the leaf,
and on the piercings made every moment by the riddling
arrows of light, all printed in the negative dough of the
void, so there is nothing now that does not leave its print,
every possible print of every possible thing, and together
every transformation of these prints, instant by instant, so
the pimple growing on a caliph's nose or the soap bubble
resting on a laundress's bosom changes the general form of
space in all its dimensions."*

There's Plenty of Time for Eternity

Physical change happened for billions of years before any
conscious being evolved. What we perceive is classified
as past or present based on our instinctual ability to
understand the directionality of entropy. This relativistic
compartmentalization of perceptions of change into
past and future is the basis of the perceptual concept
we call time. The rhythm of breathing and the day/
night cycle were likely the basis of early units of time
built into our instinctual time-labeling circuits. Neural
structuresmemories—mediating new energy patterns are
formed from perceptions. Without perception, of course,
there is change, but there is not time. Time is purely a
labeling system that has evolved in our brains.

This ability to construe time is greatly expanded and
abstracted in humans. When a paleontologist studies a
series of fossils, they know from the ages of layers in the
geological record that, for example,
the lineage of fish fossils they are
viewing ended about 20 million
years ago, because the species went
extinct 20 million years ago. They also know that it started
about 80 million years ago, and how it changed.

**Time is purely a label-
ing system that has
evolved in our brains.**

The complex mind places physical indicators of patterned change into a directional system of relative numbers—time. The time periods are known because of previous detailed studies. Simple sentient's (such as worm's) nervous systems perceive change when, for instance, a seasonal difference in light and/or temperature intensity causes them to hibernate. This hibernation represents a response to a perception of a before/after physical change in the outside world. There is probably no time perception here, though; that ability probably starts with higher reptiles, birds and mammals.

There is no need for any non-perception-dependent explanation of time in our cosmogeny. We will find that perception eventually produces eternity. For the paleontologist –who deals with local, one-time events and patterns—time works perfectly. For physicists –who try to discover universal principles—the concept of time is too provincial. In theoretical physics, it is best instead to use the concept of change based on the thermodynamic law of entropy.

12

Instantaneous Gravitation

It is possible that Isaac Newton had the intuition that the universe is infinite and that gravity acting instantaneously follows from this. In *De gravitatione*, Newton wrote that an "infinite and eternal" divine power coexists with space, which "extends infinitely in all directions" and "is eternal in duration." We now know mathematically—from Cantor—that the infinite universe produces timeless sets of every physically possible object and situation. It follows that the specific gravity of every physically separate object or situation in the infinite universe makes an infinite set when taken as a whole with its the infinite number of identical set members.

We also know from Mandelbrot that fractal geometry may make it possible that everything is in gravitational communication with everything else, as a metaproperty of infinite sets. Set theory applied to nature indicates that all infinities are in direct physical contact because they are parts of one another. For example, in one of the subatomic particles of one of the protons of a sulfur atom of a protein molecule in my body, there may exist a very large, but not infinite, set of big bang units that make up the structure— at a certain size level—of the subatomic particle.

From the view of an observer on a planet within one of these units, the unit itself seems to be 'The Universe'. This would obviously be incorrect. Physicists may someday observe subatomic particles from within.

All atoms appear to contain infinite matter and energy within them as a consequence of infinite pattern equivalence and size relativity. This may be what we call gravity. The differential pull, depending on relative amount of matter, could possibly be explained by the interaction of differential infinities—your body contains relatively 'more' and 'larger' infinites than an atom, so the earth pulls it more strongly.

What is 'The Universe'?

We once thought our galaxy was 'The Universe'. Galileo first discovered that the Milky Way was made up of countless stars in 1610. In the 1920s Edwin Hubble found

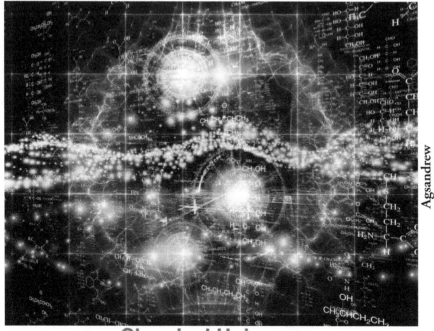

Chemical Universe

Agsandrew

out that the spots of light farther out from the Milky Way are galaxies similar to ours. The currently visible universe is likely the same. In every era, mainstream scientists tend to fall into the same trap. 'This is The Universe… oh, wait.' First, the earth and visible stars were the universe; then our milky way galaxy was discovered and became the universe. In our era, what appears to have come from the Big Bang—the visible universe—is loosely defined as The Universe.

You can see that the term 'universe' is being defined by our limitations in order to have a convenient working limit, but this is against Copernican logic. The temptation to arbitrarily set a be all, end all limit, from which to explain the entire universe, is very strong; and basing this limit on the frontiers of current technology—infrared and radio space telescopes, and so on—makes it difficult for the layman to refute. Gross physical movements of particles and energy are assumed to be adequate to elucidate universal causation mechanisms. This is good enough to explain occurrences at a simple physical level, at least as local occurrences, but not to tell us the origin or fate of the universe.

The term 'universe' is being defined by our limitations.

One Universe—Infinite Manifestations

There is no other logical possibility except that the universe is infinite. The science shows that we are in a mass of galaxies and galactic clusters where each is moving farther away from the others. However, contrary to the mainstream assumption that the visible part of universe is the entire universe, we cannot in good scientific and logical faith go along with this. From the principle of infinite particulate—quantum—reality, we have to think of the expanding area we are in as being one of a countless number. In the same way that a complex group of molecules makes up a cell, an ostrich, or a book, our particle may help make up a much larger and more complex structure.

Some have called the possibility of the universe being infinite a tragedy, but the infinite universe is a liberating and self-affirming adventure that provides eternal meaning. There is no need to force all matter into an infinitely small point, as modern physics does with the Big Bang. The most elegant of all possibilitie—the existence of a single infinite universe containing infinite iterations of all possible combinations of physical situations —is breathtaking.

Let us not sweep all matter into a crunchy point under an infinitely small rug to assuage that most gluttonous of all human concepts—time. If we do not succumb to our anthropocentric need for absolute beginnings and endings, we start to see that there is really no contradiction between the concurrent existence of infinite worlds and finite worlds.

There are currently no scientific methods to prove whether the universe is finite or infinite. For some reason, however, having to do with the preconceived difficulty of grasping the implications of true ∞, infinite universe theories have not been developed as much as they should have been. There are cases of cosmologists who say the universe may be infinite, or even that it most likely is, but who formally theorize as if it is finite anyway for their own convenience.

The Multiversal Fabric of Reality

David Deutsch, one of the main figures in multiverse theory, says in *The Fabric of Reality*:

> *A remark about terminology. The word 'universe' has traditionally been used to mean 'the whole of physical reality'. In that sense, there can be at most one universe. We could stick to that definition, and say that the entity we have been accustomed to calling 'the universe' —namely, all the directly perceptible matter and energy around us, and the surrounding space—is not the whole universe after all, but only a small portion of it.*

> *Then we should have to invent a new name for that small, tangible portion. But most physicists prefer to carry on using the word 'universe' to denote the same entity that has always been denoted, even though that entity turns out to be only a small part of physical reality. A new word —multiverse—has been coined to denote physical reality as a whole.*

He is partially right, but this thinking—partitioning unknown phenomena into some undefined and otherworldly difference from 'our universe' is anti-Copernican. It can be compared to the way naturalists before Pasteur claimed that life sprang constantly from inanimate matter in some intangible way, and even to how medieval people partitioned Heaven and Hell into intangible other worlds. Your body, and the trillions of atoms it is made of, are part of the universe, the subatomic particles those atoms are made of are parts of the universe, and so on, ad infinitum.

13

Cosmogeny & Consciousness

Man, as the minister of nature, does and understands as much as his observations on the order of nature, either with regard tothings or the mind, permit him, and neither knows nor is capable of more.

Francis Bacon
Novum Organum–1620

We will take the physical laws revealed by science so far, and those to come, to be sufficient to explain the behavior of infinite levels of emergent properties and eternal existence. The scientific method has given us the factual basis for our system of categorizing infinities. With this system we can describe and quantize eternity with predictive power in the real world.

Humans are made of atoms, molecules and biological tissues, but, understandably, a lot of people don't like to think of themselves this way. From the spiritual/religious point of view, our true nature exists at a 'higher', more meaningful level than everyday life. This is true, but the spiritually meaningful level is built of atoms, molecules and interacting biological tissues. The base materials of life are much more complex than most people can imagine, and when they interact they make things happen that are immeasurably meaningful—even spiritual. Spirituality has an origin in the physical world, and science is far enough along to start working toward a theory of eternal consciousness. Mindless anti-religious beliefs have no justification in science, and mindless anti-science beliefs have no justification in religion.

To begin to understand eternal consciousness scientifically, it is important to know what the basic **The properties of atoms** structures of life are and to **and molecules give us** connect them to quantum effects **insight into the origin** in physics; and then to connect **and functions of life.** the results with cosmogeny. We will start by concerning ourselves with the properties of atoms and molecules and how they give us insight into the origin and functions of life through molecular biology and protein chemistry.

Cosmogeny and Chemistry

Atoms and molecules were discovered by trial and error through many decades of lab experiments and observations. Real particles much too small to see were first hypothesized as logical interpretations of observations; then, after painstaking experiments, models were developed that made impressive predictions and gave results in the 'real' world of human perception.

Scientists knew there were particles with specific identities and properties that caused the laboratory reactions. They gradually refined the idea until it almost exactly matched realit—without ever seeing atoms or molecules.

The discovery of the structure of benzene, mentioned earlier, is a great example of this. In fact, advances in atomic-force microscopy have allowed us to take pictures of molecules, and these pictures show that the molecular orbital models chemists developed decades ago look exactly like the real molecules! This is similar to how there was something very real in the knowledge maps gave people in the past—and then we invented satellite imaging.

Organic molecules are frameworks made of carbon atoms, which form the basic structures of all life forms. The bonds between carbon atoms are about 120–150 picometers, a picometer being one trillionth of a meter. To give you a feeling of how small this is, over 1.5 million six-carbon rings would fit end to end within the period at the end of this sentence.

All living beings are made up of organic molecules, which are patterns of bonded carbon atoms with attached hydrogen, oxygen, nitrogen and sulfur and a few other types of atoms. The following figures shows the organic functional groups that make the foundations of all life and consciousness.

As microscopy improves, we should see molecules and atoms in more and more detail. The principles we discuss in this book may prove to have the same type of pattern-predictive ability about eternal consciousness as the principles chemists used to discover the structures of molecules. Many ancient intuitions about the larger-scale properties of the universe and consciousness were of the same nature as the intuitions of the first chemists about the nature and behaviors of molecules. Some of this ancient wisdom about spiritual or metaphysical matters may eventually be modernized and expanded on until it is understood as objectively real as well.

Organic molecules are frameworks made of carbon atoms, which form the basic structures of all life forms.

Cosmogenic Biology

In biology, higher-order molecular patterns are the primary units of importance. For our biologically based discussion, atoms and molecules can be thought of as patterns of electron energy; and higher order patterns are based on these fundamental ones. Science has given us a solid understanding of the biologically relevant properties

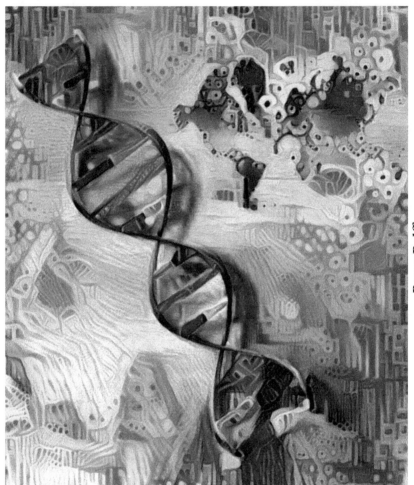

Bruce Rolff

DNA—Strand of Life

of atoms and molecules. Molecular patterns combine in nature and generate higher-order—macromolecular—emergent properties.

Small molecules like adenine form nucleic acid molecules—DNA. These nucleic acids have properties exponentially more complex than the smaller molecules which bind to make them. They form genes, which are the 'plans' for all structures of your (and every other living being's body.

DNA holds the patterns to make proteins from linking amino acids together. Every physiological and physical function of your body, and of every other living being on earth, is either caused by or mediated by a protein. Twenty-one types of amino acid molecules combine to make millions of types of proteins with amazing arrays of biological abilities.

The DNA/protein level is the first step toward life from synergistic pattern complexity out of chemical subsystems. These systems become so much more than the apparently lifeless scaffolds of nucleotides and amino acids of which they are composed.

Biological science is based on physics and chemistry—atoms and molecules—but really starts at the cell level. After the cellular, we advance to neurobiology and then extend to the biogeographical level—the most comprehensive level of biology, which studies all interactions of the biosphere and the entire history of life on earth. This will inform us of the genesis and general evolutionary properties of consciousness so we can link the quantum to eternal consciousness.

Paleontology uses evidence from the distant past in the form of fossils—as well as evidence from biological and biogeographical observation—to build an invisible pyramid, a complex map that gives a description of how life patterns changed over time. One thing it shows is the increasing complexity of animals, which means more and more advanced brains over hundreds of millions of years. In this short outline we can begin to see the links in the chain from physics to chemistry, to basic physiology and life, to self-aware minds, to eternal consciousness.

14

Human Self-Organization

When I look at the starry sky, I find it small. Either I am growing, or else the universe is shrinking, unless both are happening at the same time.

—Salvador Dali

In human endeavors toward purposeful design, form follows function. A function is desired; forms are then hypothesized and built to carry out that function. These forms are optimized by a process of trial and error. This is how a goal-oriented, self-directed—conscious—system produces something which it thinks will contribute to its survival and/or reproductive success. Some other animals with complex nervous systems have this ability. There is strong evidence that whales, dolphins and apes, among others, can produce objects and/or concepts using this form of self-directed learning.

Evolution

The human nervous system has evolved to the complexity of making concepts about the very existence and nature of concepts themselves. Our ability to produce philosophy, art and religious thought on one hand, and brutality and war on the other, led William Blake to characterize us as halfway between apes and angels—a being beginning to transcend the animal world of narrow focus on biological instinct and enter the metapattern world that lies beyond. This may have been unfair to apes, but our ability to put ourselves mentally into the shoes of other sentients— and to empathize with others—is

The human nervous system has evolved to the complexity of making concepts about the very existence and nature of concepts themselves.

the evolutionary mechanism that will enable us to enter realms of infinite conscious experience and travel through them with the freedom of eternity.

Our concept of form following function is the opposite of what happens in most of nature. In processes which are not goal directed—by a consciousness—function follows form. Evolution is the process of trial and error that happens unconsciously in nature. A system withstands and persists in an environment if it has suitable physical properties. If the complexity of this system is increased, by chance combination with another system, it can often perform more complex functions as a result of synergy. Evolved forms can be as simple as a proton or a macromolecule, or as complex as a tree, a mammal or a galaxy.

Pattern Recognition in Evolutionary Processes

All living things with a nervous system, from earthworms to whales and humans, create their own cosmos, with their particular perceptual apparatus and nervous system, from stimuli from the outside world. The structures and functions of sense organs are determined by the properties of organic molecules, and the cells and tissues they form. . Biogeographical conditions and evolutionary histories sculpt these basic materials into unique, complex lineages of life over eons. In addition, because of the huge genetic and environmental diversity within a single species, each individual lives in a mental world that is unique even in comparison with others of its kind.

However, there are commonalities in the perceptual apparatus of all animal groups which strongly indicate that they arise from fundamental energy processes. These processes directly inform conceptual intuitions about intangible aspects of the universe—our bodies and our lives are, after all, formed from atoms and their energy transactions, so we should have no concerns about discovering ways to use more 'primitive' senses to gather data on the deeper physical structure of the universe.

This supports the earlier observation that cultures through history have come upon the same ideas about unseen aspects of existence. We sense the effects of atoms and energy directly and get intuitions from them, because we have evolved from the atomic level through all simpler forms of consciousness, and contain and exist at all levels. Intuition literally means 'learning from within' and is commonly thought of as people getting knowledge about the world from instinct, which could also be called metaperception—getting information from higher order perceptual mechanisms.

Data-driven science puts raw sense information through the filters of the symbolic part of the mind, which is dependent on the limitations and subjectivity of language. It can become estranged from basic realities by these obstacles. On the other hand, fundamental instinctual perceptual abilities like the recognition of water or eyespots, for example, are based on neural structures. These structures use many pattern recognition circuits that respond to even more basic pattern elements—parallel lines, circles, color, extreme contrast, and so on) These structures use raw data from the senses to glean large-scale attributes of matter outside their bodies. All perceptual and nervous mechanisms, no matter how complex, flow from the properties of a few types of atoms—carbon, oxygen, hydrogen and nitrogen along with a few others. So, do not belittle the transcendent grandeur of atoms—you are made of them!

Synergies create emergent properties which are vastly more complex than any of their isolated components. All properties of consciousness are based upon fundamental physical structures and mechanisms, and this causes perceptions that arise directly from physical stimuli in the environment. This direct connection of consciousness to the physical world at all levels should reduce our traditional doubts about using our so-called 'subjective' senses to gather data on the deeper physical structures of the universe which are usually called metaphysical or spiritual.

Synergies create emergent properties which are vastly more complex than any of their isolated components.

The Direction of Evolution

Lancelets are primitive aquatic animals that resemble extremely simplified, blind fish. Zoologists consider them similar to the vertebrate common ancestor that evolved from invertebrates. A simple biological pattern recognition system, such as this one has, was one of the first directional nervous system types. Knowing front from rear enabled them to flee danger and move toward food and mates, rather than drifting at random and having things happen by chance like even more primitive animals such as jellyfish and sponges do. This self-direction consequently enabled the evolution of complex nervous systems that could make more and more complex choices about their own actions—and we have been running to and from things with ever-increasing passion and intensity ever since! Pattern recognition abilities expanding into what we think of as intuition blazed the trail into this frontier.

Of course, in higher mammals, especially humans, this direct sensing is mediated strongly by higher brain functions which heavily censor stimuli and attach symbolic filters to them to simplify action in the everyday world of survival. However, the raw data is available to the brain and can be accessed after training the mind to bypass the survival and reproductive filters. We can do this when we understand and take seriously the consequences of the universal principle of pattern equivalence.

The pattern recognition circuits of the nervous system are based on neural structures which use raw data from the senses to know things about large-scale attributes of matter and energy outside of their bodies. A bird, for example, can recognize water from thousands of feet in the air and decide to land in a lake. It is often argued that this is 'simply' a hard-wired reflex, followed mindlessly. This may be true, but, in our case, we use our self-awareness to redirect these types of sensory data about the universe around us into reasoning in the form of scientific hypotheses. We may then work this into theories and laws, and we use the results for technological evolution. What has been called 'intuition' for millennia is a form of this pattern recognition coming out of higher levels of emergent properties of our nervous systems.

15

Subjectivity & Survival

Our biological perceptual systems let us act separately from the 'rest of the universe'. They give us the focus to carry out individual biological activities of survival and reproduction—life must continue for consciousness to evolve. This was sensed by the ancients and explained as a deity separating itself into many other beings, sometimes just to have someone to talk to! Sentience can be characterized as the subjective creation of duality from unity: a compartmentalization. We choose which stimuli to focus on and what to think about them, within the constraints of our neural apparatus. It is this way because physical laws acting over hundreds of millions of years produced physiological structures that worked, and this led to complex autonomous beings.

Your mind is a real thing, but it is a function of molecular laws.

We will work from the premise that for the infinite and eternal existence of a consciousness, it is the totality of your subjective perceptions and apperceptions, coming from the objective physical basis, which is the fundamental unit of reality. Your mind is a real thing, but it is a function of molecular laws. Both the subjective and objective are critical to make 'the cosmos' because without mindless physical material and laws there would be no minds; and without perception and minds, there would be no meaningful 'universe' to speak of.

It is all still there without a perceiving being of course, it just does not mean anything. Before consciousness it was electrons, atoms and molecules bouncing around; at most it was a building up of biochemical complexity and of primitive life. Consciousness eventually arose from this, and that consciousness then created meaning within its neural circuits. The perceptions and apperceptions of each individual being give meaning and value to the universe, so that the individual is in effect the creator of their own cosmos. This wonder is passed on by genetics through the epochs of life on earth.

The Physical Wave and Energy

With a classic physical wave, the perceived identity depends on amplitude and frequency. Depending on frequency, waves are placed in different identity categories—visible light, gamma rays, radio waves, and so on. This shows the magnitude of perceptual difference that can be caused by a seemingly small difference in a simple property at a lower level of physical complexity.

At the higher order of human perceptual mechanisms, extremely complex biochemical reaction cascades within single neurons are activated and the networking of thousands of neurons is stimulated. The complexity of what we call perception is at least many tens of thousands of times more complex than the stimulus, and it cannot be reduced and dismissed as just a large number

The complexity of what we call perception is at least many tens of thousands of times more complex than the stimulus.

of simple reactions. These properties of consciousness –
perception, apperception, and cognition—have become
an entirely different thing. They area quantum unit which
creates meaning, and then and self-motivation based on
that meaning.

One wavelength of energy is perceived as a color by
a human eye and brain—light waves. The other is not
directly perceptible—radio waves. Some stimuli are out of
our evolved perceptual range. Of course, we discovered
radio waves and developed detection instruments for
them over one hundred years ago, so . **Some stimuli**
it is possible to discover phenomena **are out of our**
beyond our perceptual abilities. We do **evolved per-**
this by applying conceptual techniques **ceptual range.**
to observational data. The difference in
wavelength is the only thing that makes
us classify one as light and the other as radio waves. Our
evolved mode of perception 'creates' light, in the sense that
it differentiates it from other waves, complexifies it many-
fold and gleans perceptual information about the outside
world from it. We create something useful from the simple
physical movements of waves and molecules; but do not
confuse this with the naïve pseudo-philosophical idea that
our consciousness creates reality itself.

Sets of Perception

Perceptions and apperceptions are separate 'objects'
themselves, patterns of neural connections only existing
in our nervous system. The perceptual regime of humans
and the mechanisms of eternal consciousness that they
cause us to take part in are delineated by general biological
species patterns and individual genetic differences. These
give us the boundary between the absolute ∞ of all

possibilities and a merely species or individually delimited
∞.This is a relatively smaller ∞ the subset of absolute ∞,
which comprises all physically possible experiences open to
an individual, limited by their species and personal pattern
structures—a custom combo of the two non-absolute ∞ types.

As we look at how biological systems function, we
see that the complexity and range of emergent properties
increases exponentially at each level. Macromolecules
interact in complex ways and form polymacromolecular
systems—chromosomes, cell organelles, cell walls, and so
on. These then interact to create the emergent properties of
cells. The biological cell—plant, animal, fungal or bacterial—
is the basic unit, the starting point of life—Schwann's Cell
Theory. Cells congregate and aggregate into tissues; tissues
form organs; organs interact as members of systems; many
organ systems working together produce a living organism.
Many organisms of the same type make a population and,
in turn, many organisms of different types living in close
interaction with one another and the environment make
an ecosystem. Even within a level of emergence, massive
differences exist: think of the capabilities of a neuron
compared to a muscle cell or skin cell.

The differences are produced by the same old atoms
and molecules that don't appear to have any connection
to a 'soul' to many people—but look at all the wonders
that come out of the black box of emergent properties! The
old saying 'the ghost in the machine' turns out to be our
perception of the effect of what everything does together.
Consciousness, an emergent property at the organ system
level, comes from: macromolecules–>macromolecular
structures–>cells –>brain subparts—hippocampus,
cerebellum, pons cerebrum}–>brain.

16

Quanta & Qualia

The concepts of quanta and qualia are basic to what pattern equivalence means specifically for consciousness. Quanta are discrete objects and processes of every type, at every size and complexity level. They are fundamental pattern units of reality. They exist objectively—outside of a nervous system. Qualia on the other hand are mental objects formed by a nervous system –perceptions of quanta. Qualia are unique to the individual being, but they can represent real quanta closely enough to be standardized sufficiently; they can then become useable reflections of reality with which to reason with other beings. Notice that qualia are also real objects –complex brain circuits – but only exist within the nervous system.

Quanta are fundamental pattern units of reality. They exist objectively—outside of a nervous system.

Quanta

Quantum—plural quanta—comes from the Latin quantus meaning 'how much'. Quantum physics is the science that deals with the various energy levels of electrons and other particles. Quanta are energy levels that are specific to the structure of each type of particle, atom or molecule. In atoms, electrons orbit the nucleus at differing distances, forming well-defined 'shells'. These shells take on different shapes and properties depending on their positions and interactions with other shells. Chemical elements exist as quantum identities because the number and shapes of the unique orbital shells of the electrons define the specific atom.

When the configurations of the constituent electrons change, the identity changes. An atom becomes a different isotope, anion, or even another element completely, with a different electron configuration and different chemical properties. A molecule is formed by the sharing of electrons and bonding between atoms. When such a change happens, the starting unit does not exist anymore—it has become something else, formed a new quantum identity.

Perception

Everyday perceptions of the world come from the behavior of electrons. When we feel an object, we feel pressure. This happens because our nerves are made of molecules, which are made of atoms, which are electron orbital patterns. These orbital patterns are unique to specific atoms. The difference between an oxygen atom and an iron atom is determined by the number and interactions of electrons which make up the atomic orbital patterns of the specific atom. The hardness of an iron object is felt because iron atoms bond to trillions of other iron atoms with their electron orbitals to make a hard substance that moves the molecules in your nerves; and you feel that as a pressure quale.

Oxygen is the atom type—element—that our bodies use to produce energy to live and to function. It floats freely through the atmosphere and flows into our lungs because its unique electron orbital pattern causes it to bond only to one other oxygen atom and exist as a gas at standard temperatures and pressures. Once inside the body, the molecular orbitals of oxygen cause it to bond to one of the molecule types of the blood called hemoglobin. The atom in hemoglobin that binds to oxygen in order to transport the oxygen to where it is needed in the body happens to be iron. Iron is incorporated into this molecule and is physiologically active because of another physical property of its orbitals—it is easily turned into a positively charged, individual particle (a cation) by acids.

It is the same thing with all chemical elements. What we experience through other senses, such as smell and taste, comes from the same general mechanism. The unique smell of iodine or the taste of copper, for example, also come from the specific electron orbital patterns of these elements. The interactions and overlaps of atomic orbitals, through our nerves, give us perceptions—qualia—of differing smells and tastes, such as of water, sugar, vinegar or salt. We sense quantum effects through our nerves.

Through our eyes and optic nerves we sense quantum effects in a different way than our tongues. Electrons can cause action over a distance by emitting light which enters our eyes. An electron in an atom can move to a different orbital level—shell—and emit light. When this happens, the energy of the electron changes and, for some reason, a photon is released. The sun makes light this way from fusing hydrogen atoms—merging their orbitals together.

Photons are the units of light and other types of energy on the electromagnetic spectrum.

Photons are the units of light and other types of energy on the electromagnetic spectrum. Electrons can also emit other types of radiation besides light. Gamma, microwave and other wavelengths of radiation cannot be directly sensed but can be detected by instruments that humans have invented.

Electromagnetic Spectrum

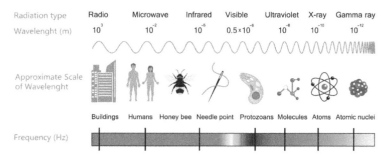

Electromagnetic Spectrum

Electromagnetic Spectrum

Photons are also reflected by the orbitals of atoms making up objects. The color that a photon appears to be to us is determined by the wavelength change after it bounces off the orbitals of the object's atoms. Photons of some wavelengths are absorbed and some are reflected. Yes, the quantum behavior of electrons causes the different colors we see. Let us say you are looking at a shiny new penny.

The color that a photon appears to be to us is determined by the wavelength change after it bounces off the orbitals of the object's atoms.

A mixture of photons reflected from the copper atoms' orbitals enters your eyes. These photons have a mixture of wavelengths that your brain experiences as yellow and red. This mixture produces the experience of a copper color.

Because of their unique physical properties, the copper orbitals reflect only these wavelengths and absorb all others. Colors are a quantum effect; photons can only be at one particular wavelength at any given time. Their energy is quantized and is expressed as a wavelength—how far each wave crest is from the next. Photons are quantum entities because each one carries an exact amount of energy and shows discrete properties such as a wavelength, frequency and energy level which are quantized as exact numbers. For example, photons produce orange light when they are moving in the wavelength range of 590–620 nanometers and at an energy between 2.0–2.10 electron volts.

Because quantum mechanical objects operate on such a tiny scale and are so different from our everyday experience, they are often used to support mystical, but dubious, ideas by non-specialists—and sometimes by specialists too! You see now that we experience quantum effects everywhere and all the time; and we are going to use everyday logic to explain quantum mechanics for our purpose of infusing eternity into everyday matter.

17

Energy & Existence

Physicists use a simple equation to calculate the energy difference when a particle moves between energy levels that are open to it when it is limited to moving in one dimension. Then another equation gives us the wavelength of the energy released. The wavelength is the distance between the crests of neighboring waves and tells us what type of energy is release—infrared, visible light, ultraviolet, radio, microwave.

This gets more interesting for us when we look at calculations for objects larger than electrons. The results of the same equation for a benzene molecule moving over a length of about 6 times the diameter of the molecule gives us a wavelength of over 9600 miles! The energy released is much too small to be measured. The diameter of benzene is hundreds of millions of times larger than that of an electron, and it is hundreds of thousands of times heavier. Remember that molecules still show quantum effects in experiments, so there is a relatively large range where we can see quantum effects.

The Universe in a Pebble

Now for the really interesting part: when we calculate the wavelength of energy released by a small stone, weighing one gram, shifting to its next quantum energy level while confined to a 10cm box, we get a wavelength longer than the visible universe! However, the energy released is so minute, we will probably never develop instruments sensitive enough to measure it.

Potter

Universe in a Pebble

This brings up interesting philosophical and scientific questions, including the question of what it would even mean for an everyday visible object like a pebble to shift to another quantum level and release a signal of this tremendous wavelength. Is it actually possible for macroscopic objects to release electromagnetic energy in the same sense as atoms do? Or does this mechanism simply not exist when we get to a certain size? We can accept that electrons, atoms and molecules are so small compared to macroscopic objects that they are subject to very different physical laws and give off energy from within that somehow moves vast distances at incredible speeds. We have a much harder time imagining how everyday objects could do something similar.

This contrast brings us to very fruitful ground for questions about the root meaning of quantum energy levels and quanta themselves. Physicists simply say we 'cannot detect quantization' in the pebble system. This may be from simple lack of instrumental resolution and it gives us a great opportunity for hypothesizing on quantum behavior of everyday objects in the infinite universe. Could the wavelength of the energy given off by the pebble shifting quantum level represent some possible connection between identical versions of the pebble—if they exist throughout the infinite universe?

That the theoretical wavelength is longer than the visible universe is a sign that the universe is potentially much bigger than we can currently see. The fact that the theoretical wavelength is longer than the visible universe is a sign that the universe is potentially much bigger than we can currently see. Perhaps a release of energy at such a long wavelength indicates some existential overlap of identical macroscopic objects? If this wavelength represents the incomprehensible distance between identical objects—like the peaks of a wave, could the minuscule energy represent the near-impossibility of their ever meeting physically?

Think of the opposite extreme with the huge amount of energy released by atoms in a nuclear explosion where identicals—atoms—the quantum increases, the wavelength approaches ∞, while the energy release approaches zero. And as the object gets smaller, the energy approaches ∞, while the wavelength approaches zero. Could this be evidence that infinite matter and energy might exist within finite objects?

"Mysticism" of Quantum Mechanics

Quantum mechanics deals with quantum objects represented by wave functions. These functions, they say, exist as a superposition or a mixture of different states at one time. Imagine a water molecule once again. Some would say it exists in all its possible states—every different combination of electron positions relative to the nucleus exist at once. In other words, the oxygen atom is pointed in every possible direction at the same time. However, when the object is observed, its wave function 'collapses' into one state according to quantum physics. A fundamental truth is being observed here, but it is crippled by limited conceptual foundations. The superposition principle of quantum physics, where a single subatomic particle seems to exist in all possible conformations at the same time, is well established. This is because they have wave properties such as interference, even though they are usually thought of as particles.

The apparent 'superposition' is caused by the property of identity. This phenomenon is often used to support mystical ideas and physics calls this quantum mysticism— but there is no reason to mystify this simple effect of quantum identity.

The superposition shown in the interference pattern of the famous double-slit experiment works with particles even at the molecular level. Organic molecules all the way up to about 70 carbon atoms have been shown to give the same results as photons and electrons in this experiment. Organic molecules will be our link from the quantum level to the everyday life level. There is no need for mysticism.

18

What Is An "Object"?

We need to be clear on the definition of 'object'. Qualia can indicate complex, intangible objects. Is the sky or even a section of it an object? To a meteorologist, it is. Is a thought an object? To a neurologist, it is—a pattern of neurons that forms particular chemical & electrical signal paths) A population of bacteria, a mental illness –these are objects to a microbiologist and a psychiatrist.

Consciously chosen pattern groups are real objects, even if they are not particles like those studied in physics and chemistry. They have definable physical structure, characteristic energy flows and unique causes and effects. A population of bacteria grows according to a unique DNA sequence and may excrete a characteristic poison molecule that kills a competitor in its environment. The specific properties of a section of atmosphere may cause a tornado to form. A mental illness may be seen as a patterning of neurons or neurotransmitter excretion that causes difficulties for the patient and which can be remedied by changing that pattern to a more comfortable one. Qualia can be categorized, but in everyday life they are often only observed as unique cases.

By contrast, the qualia studied by particle physicists and chemists are better thought of as identical to one another –as quantum objects. All carbon 14 atoms have the exact same properties. They always show us the exact same qualia. This may just be because methods are currently too limited to see the finer patterns that form those particles. They may show individual properties under high enough resolution—who knows?

The visible 'universe' of astrophysicists is even treated as a quale by many, but is this valid? It will likely change when the James Webb Telescope, which will see significantly farther than anything before it, begins operation and shows higher-order pattern structures and processes in an expanded known universe. NASA assumes that the predictions of mainstream cosmology will be found by the Webb telescope and that we will likely see the 'beginning of the universe'.

Unfortunately for this hope, there is a mismatch between measurements of the expansion rate of the nearby part of the visible universe and the distant part. They call this 'the tension', and it means that new physics will have to be found to save the predictions of the expanding universe theory. You can see how the assumption of our expanding area being the entire universe is arbitrary and, instead of considering the ramifications of ∞, modern cosmology mostly prefers to think the problem is all in the details and not in the foundation.

You can see that qualia can represent quanta, and that it is unclear at what size level quantum behavior stops; so where should we draw the borderline? It depends on how sensitive our instruments are and how complex we want science to get. It goes into the fundamental definition of pattern identity itself. Eventually it will lead, if not to a fusion of the categories of quanta and qualia, at least to a much larger overlap of the two. It is a philosophical and technical question that cannot be put off much longer if cosmology wants to progress.

Organization and Energy

My daughter and I were talking, and I mentioned that the batteries in our flashlight were dead. She looked at me with an amazed expression and asked, "Do batteries have life?" This surprised me at first, and my first impulse was to say, "No, they are just chemical reactions in metal containers that make electricity flow to the light bulb." I hesitated, though, because her question felt deep and might be a chance for both of us to get new insights into the basics of what life is. So, I gave it a little more thought in a spirit of creative open-mindedness. I told her that, even though they are not alive, batteries share a common property with the fundamental processes of life. Life is based on cells, which can be thought of as containers where chemical reactions happen. Cells use electricity (moving electrons) for the chemical reactions of life.

She then asked if fire also 'has life'. This seemed another insightful question. I answered that fire is a chemical reaction where an atom called oxygen attaches itself to another atom called carbon and a lot of energy is let out when they combine. This reaction is called combustion and it is the same basic reaction that life uses to make energy for itself. Life—at least most of it—uses oxygen to get energy from food. Carbon atoms in food give energy, so fire is like that. My daughter had felt an instinctual affinity to batteries and fire. The pattern recognition in her complex living mind had recognized the basis of life in these processes—the movement of electrical energy in the battery and the release of heat and light energy from fire.

The Spirit of Matter

During much of human history, complex physical and energetic patterns in nature, that were able to grow and withstand forces of change, were often seen as products of consciousness: we projected our minds onto the outside world. This is an idea known as animism—everything in nature had a 'spirit' and was made by a god, a wizard, or some other being. The hexagonal stones of the Giant's Causeway in Ireland are the result of a complex geological phenomenon of crystallization, but they were interpreted by the ancients as a path built by greater beings.

These types of explanation were common in most ancient cultures. We are attracted to complex crystallization patterns like minerals and snowflakes. Our minds flicker with a feeling of recognition, a familiarity and affinity with the patterned complexity. This is the root of the feeling we call beauty. In earlier times, it was most often interpreted as the design of a divinity. The modern scientific view is that it is a craving for complexity; and novelty acts as the evolutionary drive toward the exploration for new resources. Our nervous systems, possibly the most complex pattern system on earth, recognize themselves, recognize the meaning of our own inner pattern complexity; and we are forever exploring our relation to everything.

We are attracted to complex crystallization patterns like minerals and snowflakes.

Physicists and chemists understand that an atom or a molecule of a certain structure cannot be distinguished from another of the same type—they have identical properties. This is what makes science work: finding stable, fundamental identities of individual object types; then categorizing them and their interactions with other types in order to explain the workings of reality.

Patterns, Objects, and Identity Categories

Sets of identical and near-identical individuals of any possible physical organization create a phenomenon called pattern equivalence. A simple example is a specific type of molecule. Molecule species are discrete physical units that are, for all practical purposes, identical; they are quantum objects.

Anywhere in the universe, a water molecule is a water molecule. In human perception, water is an identity category which is independent of physical location or time. The qualia category known as water is determined by the limits of our observations and technology. There are isotopes and deuterated water—'heavy water', but these are just slightly different identities that are only perceptible with highly advanced instrumentation in a laboratory.

Anywhere in the universe, a water molecule is a water molecule.

In everyday experience, they do not impinge on the identity of water. Although they have individual physical existence, every single molecule that has the structure and properties of water is called water. It is an identity, a pattern category. This means, in real terms, that individuals of the set are any given member and also all members of the perceptual set at once.

What is identity? Fyodor Dostoevsky said in his book, *The Dream of a Ridiculous Man,* "But are such repetitions possible in the universe? Can that be nature's law? And if that is an earth there, is it the same earth as ours? Just the same poor, unhappy but dear, dear earth and beloved forever and ever? Arousing like our earth the same poignant love for herself even in the most ungrateful of her children?"

We call the standardized structural model of each of the elements that make up the world—as well as every single atom or molecule of a substance—by a collective name: iron, hydrogen, water, tryptophan, for example. These are elements and compounds of elements. They are the elementary particles of chemistry and biology. Being able to call an atom or molecule type the same name whether it is in bulk or a separate particle raises fascinating questions about individual vs. collective identity of practically identical objects.

19

Perception & Physical Reality

The means whereby to identify dead forms is Mathemati-
cal Law. The means whereby to understand livingforms
is Analogy. By these means we are enabled to distinguish
polarity and periodicity in the world.

—Oswald Spengler
The Decline of the West

This quote from Spengler points us toward the idea that the concept of a quantum in physics exists for objects like electrons and molecules because their energy levels and transactions can be exactly, mathematically defined. So, they are seen as identical and interchangeable. On the other hand, living things and other complex forms present individuality to us because synergistic complexity causes perceptible differences between individuals. These differences can be recognized, and a separate identity assigned to each member of the pattern type.

Qualia and Physical Reality

Qualia—singular quale—means 'of what kind' in Latin and is an idea used in philosophy and science to mean the internal, subjective sensations we get when our brains process sense perceptions from physical occurrences. This is a great partner for the physics concept of a quantum. Qualia complement the mathematically defined but content-challenged quantum levels with pure meaning,

Agsandrew

Consciously Indistinguishable Selves

while quanta give qualia objective structure. Qualia are used by scientists to tell them what things are and maybe even what they mean. For instance, the qualia of lead melting when heated enough is experienced by people all around the world. They can use a calibrated thermometer to observe that this happens at the same temperature as every other objective observersees it.

The more they are studied, the more qualia take us closer to the physical realities of the world. At the level of personal perception, we use qualia every day to make decisions. The quantum effect

At the level of personal perception, we use qualia every day to make decisions.

of color produces qualia when photons enter our eyes and

their particular-wavelength signals are processed by our optic nerve and the visual cortex of our brain. Our higher brain areas can then judge what the meaning of the color is to our survival prospects. You dot want to eat the green bread.

We can classify qualia according to complexity and build a hierarchy—from the most fundamental to the most complex yet perceived. The most fundamental level could be represented, for example, by the perception by a basic neural circuit of a directional movement, a horizontal line or a round shape. The next level of qualia would be more complex perceptions of things like the relative speeds of several objects, water surfaces and eyespots.

On the other end of the scale, we have qualia so complex that many were considered sorcery or divine action in the past, before science broke them down and explained them. Things like weather extremes, mental illnesses, and life itself in all its mystery were considered supernatural for most of our time on Earth. We have detailed scientific explanations for all of these now, but of course explanations are not realities—and no one should let them take the wonder and meaning out of existence. There are still endless frontiers to explore, and science will never find a final explanation for ultimate reality. People still perceive inexplicable spiritual events and even the divine, and probably always will.

Science and the Senses

The sciences are separated into general fields, based on complex qualia, because that is the way we sense things.

For us to be able to perceive objects and processes they need to have properties that we can observe, classify and measure. This is the idea of objects being definable as countable units, which are required to have a unique structure and unique properties to qualify as members of that class of quale—for example, proton, carbon atom, adenine molecule, mitochondria, animal cell, species member, star, galaxy, and so on.

This is the basic principle that gives separate, objective existence to the constituents of our perceptible cosmos. We sense real things in the universe, but they are greatly

The role of science is to work out the best approximations to the underlying reality that we can using the human perceptual system.

simplified and somewhat distorted by our perceptual apparatus. The role of science is to work out the best approximations to the underlying reality that we can using the human perceptual system.

Of course, a proton is a quantum unit; but the human perception of the data that prove and describe it constitute a qualia category. It is this way because we cannot directly sense quantum units. Subjectivity obviously causes variations in the interpretations made by observers, and this becomes more of a factor the more complex the qualia and their interactions are. Science is the process of working out these differences and coming to a consensus view of various objective aspects of reality.

We know that everything we see, hear and feel comes from the properties of atom and photons, but to think of everything as physics is unworkable. In science, this attitude is called reductionism and it can lead to oversimplification and dead ends.

To a working physical chemist, a human is a collection of complex chemical reactions, and even the biological identity as a species is irrelevant.

When we encounter another human, our view of them depends on the qualia level from which we see them. In everyday life, our mind assigns an individual identity, name and personality expectations to any given person. Our involvement with that person depends on our symbolic personal relationship. However, from the point of view of a physiologist in pure scientist mode, a human is an organismal pattern made up of many complex, interacting organ systems.

Although, to a degree, each has its own individual structure and physiology, that would only be considered if the physiologist had the need and the resources to investigate. To a working physical chemist, a human is a collection of complex chemical reactions, and even the biological identity as a species is irrelevant. So, you can see how changing the focus has the effect of increasing or decreasing individuality.

20

Fractals, Chaos Science & Pattern Identity

Fractal patterns theoretically contain an infinite volume within a finite border. When applied to quantum physics, this raises the essential question of what subatomic particles are composed of and, in turn, what those subcomponents are made of, and on and on. In the other direction, the question is what the visible universe is a part of, and so on. 'Fractal' comes from the Latin *fractus* meaning 'broken'. Benoit Mandelbrot, the main pioneer of fractals, coined the term to describe his new geometry, which massively extends Cantor's mathematical work on ∞ into the physical world. Scale relativity is the most important concept in this extension.

'Fractal' comes from the Latin *fractus* meaning 'broken'.

Ironically, it was an attempt to get rid of ∞ in some important quantum calculations that gave critical mathematical support to scale relativity. In the 1940s, top physicists including Richard Feynman and Freeman Dyson threw ∞ out while working with equations representing the interactions of electrons and protons. This solved their problems, but it had an interesting side effect: in the 1960s, it was discovered that this process, called renormalization,

worked by treating once-fixed properties like the mass
of an object as being variable depending on the size scale
it was seen from. This was an absurdity to mainstream
thinkers, but it fit perfectly with what Mandelbrot and
others studying fractal geometries were seeing. It means
that as standard masses and lengths change relative to the
observer, depending on size level, something else remains
fixed—as it must to balance the equation. This fixed
property, this constant, is the fractional dimension itself,
which is infinite—and was found to contain infinite sets of
identical objects at different size scales and masses relative
to the observer. This viewpoint eliminates problems of
scale and time in cosmology.

Fractals and Endless Complexity

In a fractal the original pattern eventually regenerates
itself from the structures built by the starting equations.
We see it re-emerge endlessly within smaller and larger
levels of complexity as the pattern evolves infinitely. It
is the common motif which seems to create the endless
complexity. In mathematics, it is often controversial to
extend the results of equations to the real world but, in this
case, we have extensive physical observations that give
strong evidence that this is how every physical system
operates. The effects of fractal geometry can be brought
into the physical world by assuming a specific starting
equation represents a quantum type and expresses the
deep structure of it.

Since the late 1970s, when the fractal dimension and
its mechanisms began to be well known, it has been
extended into practically every field and subfield of science.
In all these cases, fractal mechanisms have been shown
to accurately model processes specific to each field. The

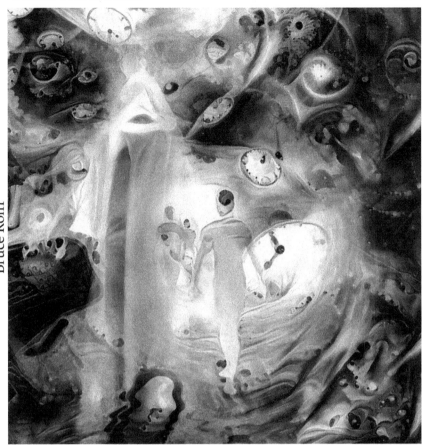

Bruce Rolff

Journey of the Self

fractal dimension is a fundamental concept of what became known as 'chaos science'. The basic pattern seen is that the behavior of complex systems occurs with periods of high organization alternating with periods of apparently complete disorganization. Is this 'disorganization' really chaos, though? Or is it just an observer effect?

Let us take an example from ecology. A messy jumble of decaying organic matter on a forest floor would be considered by a botanist to be the chaotic phase of 'highly organized' system of plants and plant communities. The decaying mess is seen as the background that living patterns emerge from. Complex beings arise from it via the influence of the organizing principle called, in chaos science, a 'strange attractor'. In this case it is the genetic codes of various plants that produce the next complexity level from materials in the decayed matter. From different points of view, it would not be chaos. The microbial ecosystem of the decaying forest floor and the biochemical reactions in, it to a microbiologist or a biochemist, are highly ordered. In this case, the actions of microbial species and their biochemical reaction mechanisms are the attractors.

Again, we see mystification caused by technical language in science. The background matter is only chaotic from the limited view point of a specific level. The attractor is 'strange' relative to the matter it acts upon because it is at a completely different level of complexity and emergent properties.

Time, Energy, and Complex Patterns

With more complex patterns, effects on time also come into play. The relative ages of patterns do not depend on the ages of their constituents. A quilt made today, from a combination of material from a 200-year-old flag and completely new material from the store, is considered a new quilt. It is a newly-made pattern; the age of the constituents doesn't interfere with its newly-formed pattern identity. Look at the skin on your arm. It is made of atoms, many of which are hundreds of millions of years old; yet you, your pattern identity, is only decades old.

We are each a complex physical pattern that creates certain repeatable energy properties, which, when taken in their totality, make up our personalities and memories.

Ten years ago, most of the molecules that formed your body

were different—water, proteins, minerals, and so on. Ten years from now, most of the molecules of your body will be different ones again; but there is a continuity: the pattern that existed and changed yet stayed fundamentally the same thing. We are each a complex physical pattern that creates certain repeatable energy properties. These, taken in their totality, make up our personalities and our memories. In our minds, the properties and identities of fundamental ingredients of a pattern are drowned out by the higher-level subjective identities that they make. It is possible to mentally drift back to the beginning and let all component levels of your existence, of your consciousness, your physical mind be sentient at once. This is to see—and be—all the trees in the forest at once and not just the forest from a distance.

21

Quantum Identity & Pattern ∞

Infinite sets of any possible physical arrangement create an emergent property called Pattern ∞. For example, let us say that every water molecule in the universe is in a different relative surrounding from any other. Differences of position and momentum of other objects relative to

Infinite sets of any possible physical arrangement create an emergent property called Pattern ∞.

a molecule and the observer are the only factors that make it an 'individual'. The relative difference is caused by the time and viewpoint limitations of the observer. It does not affect the quantum identity of the molecule.

It follows that individuality is not a quantum property, It is a relative one. Identity is localized by a conscious observer. The eternally stable quality of quantum objects is the basis for pattern ∞. Quantum objects of all types interact to form an infinite variety of individuality in the mind of an observer by relative differences in infinite movements and changes. Pattern ∞ expands the property of mentally synthesized identification of quantum actions into Cantor's Set Theory.

Archetype and Identity

An old philosophical way of describing eternal pattern identity was the archetype. The activities of quantum objects do cause changes without being observed, of course. That is how the universe evolves; but without an observer to experience subjectivity/perceptual relativity, there is no meaning. When a fossil is formed, it is merely a collection of atoms, but its image remains to be seen and interpreted later by a mind.

An old philosophical way of describing eternal pattern identity was the archetype.

With sophisticated enough instruments, a single water molecule could be differentiated from others in a solution using its relative position and movement compared to outside objects, such as other water molecules and salt ions. However, this is only a relative differentiation—an assignment of temporary individual identity entirely from the unique perspective of the observer. It is a subjective triangulation between the observer, the water molecule, and a third entity which provides a point of differentiation. The observation has no effect on the identity of the molecule. Until a chemical change happens, creating a different pattern identity—such as a breakdown to its constituent hydrogen and oxygen atoms –the identity of the molecule remains that of any and all water molecules. However, once it is observed, it 'becomes' an individual. This is the 'observer effect' of physics.

Physicists seem to want such a convenient and precise particle model as chemistry has for their own discipline. They dream of finding gravitons and even God particles; but it is not likely to happen because they do not have

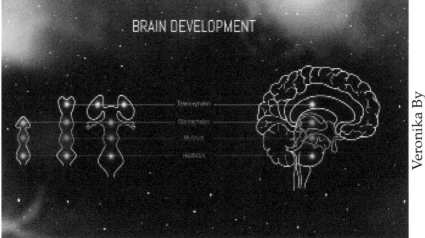

Brain Evolution

a limitation of focus to a single size scale like there is in chemistry. This problem could be solved by letting the reference point move freely to objects on an infinite spectrum both up and down the size scale and finding constants common to all size and complexity levels. This has possibly gotten off to a start with the connection of the Planck length—related to subatomic particles—to the Schwarzschild radius—related to black holes.

The "Observer Effect"

There is always some uncertainty in science, and the more complex the patterns, the more uncertainty we have to deal with. In the best of cases, with relatively clear data, statistical analysis gives us margins of error with which to judge our accuracy and precision. In physics the Heisenberg uncertainty principle takes the form of the 'observer effect'—the fact that both the position and trajectory of a particle cannot be observed at the same time. We know that all our experiences and activities in science as well as everyday life are approximations. Especially in frontier sciences, we have to be okay with some fuzziness; we have to weigh up how well our approximations reflect the reality we are trying to understand.

In the 'wave collapse' of quantum mechanics, a particle is observed to move one way or another. A new, but only subjective, quantum identity is assigned by the observer. This subjective quantum identity does not impinge upon the eternal universal identity shared by the individual particle with all infinite members of its pattern set because the 'new identity' only exists in a person's mind –it is just a new label. These types of changes are obviously not actual quantum changes. The only real change is in the mind of the observer.

A structural change creating a different chemical gives a molecule or atom a new identity. The particle 'quantum leaps' to a new identity; and an identity is a neural perception of a quantum (discrete) entity. The former identity disappears from perception locally and something new takes its place. For example, a water molecule may break into one oxygen and two hydrogen atoms. The molecule "disappears" in effect. More exotic types of local disappearance, like this one of a water molecule is what mystifies people about things like the double slit experiment quanta and gives rise to 'spooky' feelings about action-at-a-distance effects.

But remember that identity/pattern infinity is delocalized. Did Giordano Bruno feel this when he told the inquisition, "All things, souls and bodies are immortal as to their substance, nor is there any other death than dispersion and reintegration"? The motion of electrons and other subatomic particles, with their dual wave/particle behavior causes confusion because we can't instinctually grasp how they move and relate it to our everyday experience.

22

The "God Particle"

…You could then tell yourself that what you are now living you could live again better, at the same time that you were living something different… Everything which I miss living at every instant, everything that I am wasting at present, all the ineffable congealed cascades of sensation and emotion which escape me at this moment without my even being aware of it, this whole treasure of life, of time which I am losing, one day I shall find again with a fresh wonder, in a new and real terrestrial paradise.

—Salvador Dali
Fifty Secrets of Magic Craftsmanship

The study of fossils is an example of pattern recognition from information saved in the past and transmitted over millions of years. In the case of a fossil, we can use the term 'in-formation' literally: the form of a living organism was put in stone by physical processes and it is recognized as a once-living being by referring instinctually to a neural pattern model formed in the human mind through evolution.

Let us say a fossil fish in a 100 million-year-old layer of a cliff is exposed by erosion and falls into a stream face up. A wildcat happens by, whose nervous system is evolutionarily adapted to recognizing and eating fish. It sees the fossil from a distance and perceives it as a possible meal. The cat begins to carefully stalk then pounce on the 'fish'. Of course, it is confused when it realizes it has not caught any food. The 'event', to use physics terminology, that caused the change of movement of the cat was not simply movement of a physical object or an energy vector directly touching the cat's body. No object or energy outside of the cat's body pulled or pushed it in the direction of the fossil. The cat decided to move itself toward the stimulus.

What was the event that caused the movement? It is too easy to say that it was just an extremely complex series of reactions—starting from the reception of an image in the cat's eyes causing the production of a cascade of energy transactions in the nervous system—which finally made the cat's body move how it did. This is correct at a certain level, but we lose a lot through such reductionism. It is possible to go farther than the simple and immediate biological physics of the situation.

We need to think in terms of complex systems and their evolution over millions of years.

If we try to trace back to what caused this instinctual neural cascade, where does it lead us? Was it the light rays transmitting the image to the cat's eyes? Was it the fall of the fossil into the stream face up? Do we have to go back to the formation of the fossil itself to find a meaningful initial cause of the cat event? No; all of that is essential, but insufficient. We need to think in terms of complex systems and their evolution over millions of years. What if we go back to the evolution of the recognizable body plan of fish as a basic evolutionary group? Now we are getting closer. We also need to bring in the evolution of pattern recognition of a generic fish shape in cats to find the ultimate physical cause of our cat pouncing on a pattern on a rock. Looking at these two events together, we can say that a biological pattern-recognition system (the cat's brain) has produced a connection of two complex evolutionary processes that happened over 100 million years apart.

Information from entangled, complex evolutionary processes was transmitted across millions of years by an impression of a pattern in stone, linking it with a complementary, distantly co-evolved nervous system. This example shows a little of the complexity brought into the study of physical causality by a sentience.

Beyond the Human Senses

Applying this to the human mind, it gets exponentially more complex because, unlike simpler animal minds, we can make conceptual models, learn from the past, and speculate on the future. We could break this process down into any number of parts at any resolution we choose—molecular, cellular, organismal, ecological, and so on, to try to pin down a single 'event' responsible for causing the cat's fruitless hunt. We would only be limited by our conceptual and technical abilities. We could even go all the way back to the subatomic structures of the constituent atoms of DNA if we really wish to find an ultimate cause that would explain our cat/fish scenario.

Unlike simpler animal minds, we humans can make conceptual models, learn from the past, and speculate on the future.

This absolute reductionism is a recognized approach in modern physics—the concept of finding 'The God Particle'. However, this violates the universally observed expanded Copernican principle. As our technical abilities improve and we 'see' the subatomic realm at ever higher resolutions, it will become obvious that we are not in any

special position to see the endpoint of the **The very**
universe. In fact, the very concept of a **concept of**
universal limit is naïve. Science is ready **a universal**
to move past using the resolution limits **limit is naïve.**
of our senses and instruments as being
possible endpoints of the universe. Endless evolution of
pattern and metapattern relations is the way to look at
things.

Biocosmogeny & Infinite Complexity

We know that biological organisms and systems are
self-sustaining at all structural levels. This is the drive
that enables continuous, infinite self-creation and a
continuous increase in complexity. We also know that as
pattern-recognition systems work with the data of pattern
similarity, they have the ability to link events over any time
span or space distance differential using the concept of
fungible pattern identity.

Biological functions may appear, at first glance, to
be 'just' very complex chains of causation events which,
from one perspective, they are. The problem is the word
'just', because a new phenomenon—a startling emergent
property—has arisen from the existence of consciousness;
and this property causes the
recognition of the universe by   **Self-sentience of**
itself. Self-sentience of matter   **matter and energy**
and energy as a whole has been   **as a whole has been**
unleashed by biological evolution   **unleashed by biologi-**
in the infinite universe. Evolution   **cal evolution in the**
toward infinite complexity   **infinite universe.**
makes this inevitable. The
'Holomovement' of David Bohm is one such formulation of
this type of idea.

No matter how complex the movements of a physical system become, many are convinced that all events in the universe can be described and explained by conventional mechanics and quantum mechanics. This is considered to hold up even with complex creative behavior in higher animals. The predictive power of these theories breaks down at the level of higher biological sentience in its modes as self-aware infinite pattern recognition sets—sets of infinite individual minds—especially in the ability to transcend ego consciousness and articulate with other physically individual consciousnesses.

Here, we are in the territory of qualia that have become quanta. individual minds are qualia under outside observation from another mind, but are experienced in their true form by the individual mind as quanta when the reality of the mind's infinite set—the true self—is experienced from within. This is analogous to how we can conceive of an infinite set of identical water molecules, which are considered quantum units in the present scientific status quo.

23

Human Experience of Infinity

The most logical approach to begin exploring the true structure of the universe is to hypothesize that it goes on forever in both size directions in fractally-structured quantum levels. There are infinite progressions of increase in material complexity. The quantum units perceptible to science nowsubatomic particles, atoms, molecules, cells, organisms, planets, stars, galaxies, galactic clusters, galactic clouds with complex shapes and gravitational properties, Big Bang units... go on and on and on...or maybe until a functional reset is reached and these units form what we know as fundamental particles –an electron, a quark or even something much smaller. These units become fundamental particles of a larger system.

This explanation of universal structure starts from a solid definition of 'Universe' and uses a modernized Copernican principle. It provides, for our scientific study and human wonder, a truly feasible and infinite source of sentient experience and growth: pattern ∞. The most important contribution of this theory is to the subjective experience of the individual—the conscious observer. Pattern ∞ provides mechanisms by which consciousness advances to experience more comprehensive infinite situations. These advances are potentially endless in extent and complexity. Every individual consciousness, through the mechanisms of pattern ∞ in the physical and energy exchanging structures of its nervous system, eventually learns to transcend individual space and time limits to achieve experience of the totality of universal pattern.

This negates the need for creation myths that have beginnings and ends. This includes creation models based in science like the expanding universe theories and multiverse theories where 'universes' create other 'universes' which can also end. These insights may help increase the scope and predictive power of cosmology.

The Pattern of the Universe

The universe is popularly thought of as stars, galaxies, black holes, and other astronomical objects; but these are merely words for things we can currently see. The principles we have learned from the fractional dimension, combined with infinite matter, energy and space, show us that existence extends forever into the sub-microscopic as well as into the super-macroscopic realms. In the macroscopic direction, emergent property regimes increase exponentially, or possibly until the structural level resets back into a sub-atomic world.

The term 'subatomic' is a human perceptual construct. There is no physical reason the patterns with the same structure we call subatomic should not exist in larger scales. When we have the instruments to look deeply enough in the subatomic direction, we may observe patterns once more resembling what we think of as astronomical.

What makes the concept of infinite fractal size relativity difficult for many is taking human perceptual constructs as entities occupying absolute and exclusive size levels. I know that professional scientists will not be likely to make this mistake at an intellectual level, but emotions can make us unconsciously and unknowingly override logic. We tend to place ourselves in the middle of the spectrum of known size levels. We consider our views of size to be objective because they are relatively objective—from the platform of the anatomy and physiology of human perception. This is a modern type of cosmological anti-Copernicanism. It has an understandable, unconscious root, though.

Our physical bodies are subject to finite perceptions because of our finite evolutionary anatomy. Our evolutionarily useful tactic of self-assertive dominance at

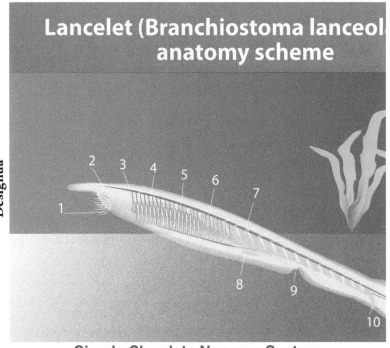

Simple Chordate Nervous System

the cost of insight is understandable as an instinctual reflex. However, surely we have evolved beyond that, haven't we?

Beyond Cosmology

We need to work from the realization that our ingrained, ancient evolutionary imperatives as physically individual organisms need to be suspended when we approach large questions about systems that are independent of our existence. The most fascinating approach is to take our perceptual platform—human senses and nervous systemas being within one size/pattern complexity level on an infinite spectrum of size and complexity levels. The universe defined in this way is already infinitely bigger and more complex and, most importantly, possesses infinitely more potential than the usual universe of modern cosmology. Size relativity is, however, just a single dimension of actual physical ∞.

Let us say that, after careful observations at higher and higher levels with more and more powerful instruments, astronomers finally map the borders of what they think is the universe. Astrophysicists compute the physical properties of the entire region of billions of galactic clusters that make up our observable universe.

Certain geometries, energy transactions and other properties turn out to be identical to those of a quark within a subatomic particle.

They study it as a particle and compute constants based on this data. Then a physicist recognizes the constants as being uncannily close to ones that have just been computed for a particular property of a sub-subatomic particle.

Certain geometries, energy transactions and other properties turn out to be identical to those of a quark within a subatomic particle. It is apparently the same as any quark studied by subatomic physicists in any regular human-scale world like ours. Can we say that we have now seen a quark? How 'big' is that quark? As big as any other of its type, because it is every other of its type within our frame of reference –the quantum unit known as a quark–remember that pattern identity is independent of surroundings.

Paradoxically, it is also as big as the space filled by billions of galaxies from our subjective relative scale. Is it part of a proton or maybe a neutron? We would have succeeded in providing the first relativistic case of a supragalactic structure doing double duty in another spatial realm as a quark. This would provide the connection between 'different universes'.

If we could go further, with even more powerful instruments, we might see that the neutron or proton is part of an oxygen atom. We research even further and discover it is part of a higher superstructure acting exactly like a water molecule. We end up realizing that we are studying subatomic physics, atomic physics and chemistry from within an actual molecule! This would be quantum theory extended to the entire infinite universe, not just subatomic particles and atoms.

Thought experiment possibilities like this show the self-imposed limits of multiverse theories. What are often called different universes are actually one universe—part of the universe we experience every day. It is also possible that there is one Big Bang unit which eternally expands and contracts and, of course, contains within every one of its atoms an ∞ of fractal existence levels. This still means an infinite universe.

24

The Universal Fractal Pattern in ∞

Theories are expected to make predictions, and Universal Fractal Pattern Infinity—UFPI—predicts that as astronomical instruments advance, if they can advance that far, we will start to see eerily familiar mathematical patterns emerge from the mysterious galactic superstructures that look random to us now. As subatomic physics and astronomical observations advance, it will be wise for physicists and astronomers to collaborate with chaos science, and to share and compare data in order to catch any of these patterns as their first signs begin to come out from behind the limits of current instrument-aided perception.

UFPI provides the mechanism for eternal time as well as timelessness, which is the another dimension of actual ∞. The two seem to be opposites that rule out the very existence of the other, but they are really sides of the same coin, or two hands clapping—insert your own Zen saying here. They look mutually exclusive to us, but they exist simultaneously because they are just effects of an infinitely scaled, infinitely repeating universe. Timelessness exists through infinite sets of identical instances of every

> UFPI provides the mechanism for eternal time as well as timelessness.

possible physical conformation occurring at every moment. Eternal time, on the other hand, exists through the infinite variety of infinite sets of physical conformations.

Timeless patterns prove that the ancient idea of archetypes was correct all along, except that an archetype is not a perfect object, just an eternal pattern. The human reality detector is a lot more precise and sensitive than it has been given credit for by reductionist science. Many other items of ancient wisdom are like this—the concept of an infinite, cyclic universe, for example. Of course, many ideas were bad, and some were horrible—like the earth-centered universe and burning witches and heretics alivebut we should not throw the baby out with this filthy bathwater. To dismiss ideas simply because they are 'ancient' is intellectually dishonest. The idea of the infinite universe is so common across so many cultures, that it has some significant weight of consensus behind it.

Much More Than "Everything"

The opinion that an infinite universe is inconceivable or too hard to theorize with comes from the incorrect idea that ∞ is simply 'everything'. Infinities can be categorized and structured mathematically and scientifically. The old concept of luminiferous ether has come back to physics in the form of zero-point vacuum energy in the void, where the void is considered a quantum system. Although this is not likely, as we have seen from Lucretius, at least they are giving old ideas another chance.

Infinities can be categorized and structured mathematically and scientifically.

The infinite creative potential of size relativity explains well how everything can come from 'nothing'—without the unlikely singularity of the Big Bang—and how infinite time can exist, yet timelessness also exists. Infinite universe theory and archetypes need to come back too. The work of Cantor, Mandelbrot and many others has earned it.

When the scale relativity interpretation of the infinite fractal universe is used to extend quantum mechanics, we get past provincial anti-Copernican limitations. We infer that what is without is within, that the phenomena we observe at the subatomic level necessarily repeat cyclically and endlessly at supra-macroscopic as well as sub-subatomic levels. Superposition—as seen in the double slit experiment—is likely the simultaneous existence of practically identical objects—'practically' referring to **Quantum identities** perceptual tolerances—at different **are human interpreta-** locations and relative scales. The **tions, they cannot** size differences of these objects **assign an absolute** are canceled out by their pattern **existence to an object.** identity. Like in an algebra equation, they are multiplied by a common denominator, their common identity, which is an archetypal property of more fundamental processes. This mathematically converts qualia to quanta, as the difference is purely a matter of perceptual scope.

Quantum identities are human interpretations, they cannot assign an absolute existence to an object. From our quark example, we may just as well call it a quark or the universe. At any rate, the actual quantum entity exists in a timeless, placeless form as a consequence of being a member of an infinite set of identical objects. It is thus in an infinite variety of subjective situations relative to an infinite variety of other object types.

The human 'object' as an observer assigns an identity based on her/his relative position. Conscious perception causes what is called a 'decoherence' in quantum physics

—assignment of a subjective identity. Any change to
an individual object, however, is inconsequential to its
archetype, because the type exists in infinite sets, and (∞ -
1= ∞). Addition to an infinite set is the same (∞ + 1= ∞)
since physical processes are reversible.

Indivi-Duality & the "You" in Universe

Consider, however, that there is an infinite set of real water
molecules in which every member exists in exactly the same
surroundings as all others of the set. We will call this its objective set. It is the same from an objective or outside point
of view. The objective set has the property of perceptual
indistinguishability. The objective set of an individual mind,
by analogy is the basic mechanism of true individuality.

This analogy is our basis for a modern scientific justification of the ancient spiritual concept of the eternal True
Self. We will see how the principle of pattern ∞, when
applied to a conscious observer instead of a molecule,
produces the most amazing results. We will call the infinite objective set for a consciousness the set of consciously
indistinguishable selves—CIS), and this corresponds to
Cantor's infinity of identicals set type.

∞ includes eternity as a subset. Eternity is a property of
∞, a consequence of the perception of infinite real sets and
their infinitely articulated connections to one another. Time
is the perception of change; perception and change are
properties of matter; infinite matter creates infinite change
and infinite perception, thus infinite time. Pattern ∞ creates
a periodicity of existence which is split between perceptual
regimes of time on one hand and eternity/timelessness
on the other. The important point to grasp is that these
regimes exist simultaneously.

25

Mind, Time & Duality

Here is a simple explanation of particle/wave duality. One aspect exists for a particular consciousness when that consciousness is focused on it. The other aspect still exists, of course, but not at that moment for that particular consciousness.

An example from human experience: imagine you are the coach of a sports team. Your team has 15 members, all of whom happen to be currently elsewhere doing personal, non-team related activities. This collection, this set of people is a pattern in your mind. The people exist of course and act in conscious ways to propagate the pattern, but the entity 'team' is really just a series of neural circuits—memories—in your mind.

You have memories of your perceptions of individual players' physical and personality properties stored in your brain which allow you to recognize and assign each individual a place in the common pattern. Your memories **Our memories** of each individual are linked together **are linked to-** into a complex set of patterns in your **gether into a** mind that you call your team. Your next **complex set** team meeting is two weeks away and, **of patterns in** as far as you could know, some team **our mind.** members may have firmly decided to quit the team and have not called you yet. One may be planning to send his/her twin brother/sister to fill in at the next practice so they can go to a party.

At any rate, you know that your team in some form will show up for the next practice. In this sense, the team is something real. In another sense, it is not. This is an illustration of the classic problem of physical duality. The wave/particle duality of subatomic particles, mentioned earlier, fits this analogy.

If a very different team shows up from the one corresponding to the pattern in your mind, you just may lose the next game. In that case, you realize, this was not the same team you thought it was! To connect this to the duality problem: there is something real there—a specific set of individuals that you know are going to gather at the same place and time and exhibit certain properties. The pattern that was created in your mind by all your previous experience with your team is also something real; it is an arrangement of neurons connected together and animated by neurotransmitters which causes you to behave a certain way in reference to the individuals and also to their behaviors as a team.

Duality

The duality of the two sets 'decoheres' when one is observed. When you begin to watch the actual team in a game, the pattern in your mind does not stay the same. It is continually modified by cognitive processing, whether conscious or unconscious. This modification is called apperception and is the way sentient beings integrate perceptions into memory patterns.

Which is more 'real'? Think about it this way: the old neural pattern still exists in memory (you can remember what you thought or expected about the situation), while the actual team and its behaviors are already something very different and can never be the same—yet most people call the physical team real. The question of which is more real is the stumbling point of the duality problem. They are both real.

In this case, one—the neural pattern—is a representation of the other—the team. In the traditional physics duality problem, the two partners are particle and wave. Think about the graphic representations of a particle—sphere—a discrete, tangible object—and a wave—undulating line—a periodic pattern). The intangible but real periodicity of waves makes them good analogies for pattern infinite phenomena.

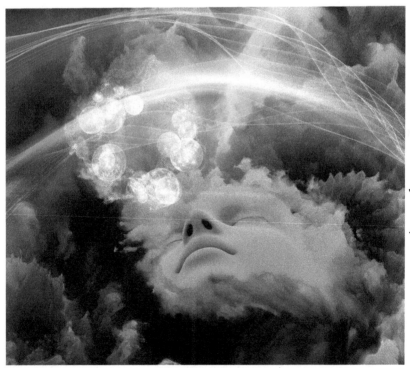

Agsandrew

Worlds Within

Identity in Infinity

All sets are infinite; and the individuals minds of a set are meta-connected—by the mind pattern—because of a very close or identical functional and structural similarity, within certain tolerances (to use an engineering term). To say that there is only one 'me' in an infinite universe is like saying that there is only one water molecule in the universe, or, conversely, that every water molecule has to have a separate name and be identified as a unique individual because it has separate, subjective properties. As a sentient pattern phenomenon, you can choose to perceive yourself as an individual or, with the proper practice, as a member of an infinite set of sentients at any resolution of differences from your individual physical self. The deciding factor is whether a pattern unit is effectively the same within the limits of perception and the relevant time frame of the observed phenomenon—a water molecule, an individual consciousness.

We have a strong biological instinct to protect our individual physical existence, which extends into the world of ideas and concepts.

Biological Instinct

That is what is relevant to consciousness, not absolutes or perfection. We have a strong biological instinct to protect our individual physical existence, and this extends strongly into the world of ideas and concepts. UFPI frees us from our individual physical boundaries, while maintaining the individual consciousness as the fundamental unit of reality. When one begins to get the feel for thinking in terms of an infinite universe and eternal pattern equivalence, the seemingly insurmountable contradictions of duality begin to disappear.

The most important contribution of this theory is to the subjective experience of the individual, the conscious observer. Pattern ∞ provides mechanisms by which consciousness advances to apprehend more comprehensive infinite pattern sets and their dynamic interactions. These advances are potentially endless in extent and complexity. Individual physical consciousness, human or otherwise, through pattern infinite functional channels, automatically transcends individual spatial and time limits to achieve the totality of universal pattern ∞ and eternity. To perceive it is a matter of finding how to turn off the symbolic mind. Possible mechanisms causing this transcendence will be laid out in the next chapter.

Higher properties emerging from matter and energy give rise to human—and others'higher consciousness and form a quantum level which, when multiplied in scope by fractal infinitude, bring molecular/energy patterns on the path toward divinity.

UFPI may also help to explain gravity and other recalcitrant phenomena by the mechanism of differentially infinite 'worlds' existing within a space traditionally defined as finite.

26

Individuality & Eternity

And I have felt a presence that disturbs me with the joy of elevated thoughts; a sense sublime of something far more deeply infused, whose dwelling is in the light of setting suns, and the round ocean, and the living air, and the blue sky, and in the mind of man... well pleased to recognize in nature and the language of the sense, the anchor of my purest thoughts, the nurse, the guide, the guardian of my heart and soul, of all my mortal being.

—Wordsworth
Lyrical Ballads

Pattern Eternity coming from Universal Fractal Pattern ∞ gives us a way to explore the physical mechanisms of eternal consciousness by integrating infinite set theory with the sciences of quantum physics and chaos. Universal pattern equivalence applied to infinite sets of conscious structures—nervous systems/minds, gives a basis for explaining and predicting 'metaphysical' phenomena of consciousness. Science provides a logical way toward the reconciliation of what are usually considered the purely physical and the purely metaphysical.

Science provides a logical way toward the reconciliation of what are usually considered the purely physical and the purely metaphysical.

The Transcendent Experience of ∞

Spiritual insights and phenomena that have been recorded through human history give us a data set of similar observations, some of which we will take to represent real physical phenomena that are still beyond our technology to observe and examine. Parapsychology is a controversial field which attempts to categorize and explain these observations; but it does not have a structure based on physics as more accepted scientific fields do. It is notable that the word parapsychology contains the word psychology. It is, of course, rooted in psychology.

Minds in certain states seem to have transcendent metapattern abilities that come from retraction of the thin symbolic layers and activation of deeper functional areas of the brain. Among other things, parapsychology studies observations that seem to come, via a living person, from the minds of people who have already passed away.

Parapsychology studies observations that seem to come, via a living person, from the minds of people who have already passed away.

A good starting hypothesis for parapsychology is that dying people in different time periods can sometimes still interact with people living in our subjectively present time. They do this by suspending subjective time with the energetic mechanisms available through the timeless connections of their metasets during the death process.

Methaphysical Occurrences

Occurrences that seem metaphysical or spiritual in nature are observed more often than many people think. However, most people do not want to tell others and look strange, or they simply ignore them out of misunderstanding or fear. Thanks to modern discoveries, explanations can be found for many widespread phenomena that are usually thought of as metaphysical. Consciousnesses are physical, and yet they transcend the physical in the sense that their metaperceptual structure is communal and negates subjective time and space. 'Subjective' in the sense that the physical basis is the local perception of a discrete individual, not in the dismissive sense of an egotistical fallacy. These differentially infinite consciousnesses, acting within the principles of Cantor's theory of transfinite sets could be called transperceptual.

Pattern ∞ can be directly perceived under certain circumstances—by all the infinite iterations of a sentient being at a certain shared moment when they happen to converge attention on one another. The mortal aspect of individual perceptual experience—caused by focus on individual biological imperatives—can be transcended. Because of this, each and every perceptual reality exists for all time. Summed up over the infinite individuals of the set, this is pattern eternity for an individual. Any single perceptual experience in your life is eternal and can be used as a starting point into larger eternal sets—sets of more comprehensive experience. The phenomenon of endless conscious existence is an effect of pattern eternity summed up over the infinite individuals of a universal set.

Pattern ∞ can be directly perceived under certain circumstances

The True Self

The individual nervous system is the fundamental unit of eternal consciousness. It is the quantum level where all existence is experienced. Without consciousness, there is no experience, only existence. Physically individual sentience is a necessary condition for infinite consciousness –a still point in the center of the chaos of the eternal experience of infinite sets of every other being. Eastern philosophies tell us of the true self, the individual mind that interacts with all other existence. They say that, once one finds and completely understands the true self, one can connect with all other existence.

Basic philosophy tells us that meaning comes from selfhood and community. Basic psychology tells us that the communication of meaning comes from common understandings between individuals of a similar type. Humans understand ideas coming from other humans— ideas that come from brain structures common to all

Basic philosophy tells us that meaning comes from selfhood and community.

humans. We are even beginning to understand how to communicate with other beings: dolphins, chimpanzees, and so on. These two principles –eternal individuality and infinite potential for communication with other selves – create eternal, ever-expanding consciousness.

Consciously Indistinguishable Selves—CIS

Identical twins have characteristics that make them eerily the same. This can be seen in the extreme similarities in interests and behaviors of twins separated at birth, including pseudo-telepathic abilities—having almost the same mind. By logical extension, an even more exact replica of you than any twin could be, in an environment which is exactly the same, is you—in the same way that the properties of the oxygen molecule make one the same as any other. These are individual selves which are so equivalent that you cannot tell them apart.

It is, currently, physically impossible to visit an identical copy of yourself somewhere else in the universe; but think of your set of selves as a force field that is always connected to you. Endless physical selves are converging and diverging to your identity at every instant, but always leaving an eternal now in its wake. In quantum field theory, the universe is thought of not as isolated particles, but as fields. The field of all matter is unified as a quantum, a single thing; and the units that make it are quarks and leptons. We can think of our CIS set in a similar way.

An individual can perceive the ∞ of their personal existence by convergence at a moment of clarity. They can become aware of the infinite CIS set of individuals in the exact same situation that they are presently in. The infinite universe provides continuously converging as well as diverging sets of CISs at every instant. There is always an infinite set of near 'yous' sharing the critical amount of molecular similarity— of body and of situation, changing into you—and also an infinite set changing away from being you—at every instant.

Individual can perceive the ∞ of their personal existence by convergence at a moment of clarity.

This generates the perception of an infinite existence of your present self at a certain moment. It is something like looking into a mirror at just the right angle and seeing endless reflections of yourself except that, in this perceptual phenomenon, you become the reality of being an infinite number of identical people at one instant. Suddenly, you are overwhelmed by the intensely real perception that the moment will last forever if you hold your perception on it in the proper way.

27

Beyond Measure & Analysis

There is a pattern infinite 'crystal' of every moment. point in time when each individual consciousness has converged on every other of the set at a particular moment of life and they all become conscious of one another. Something happens, at these moments, which connects consciousnesses so far apart that it is impossible

There is a pattern infinite 'crystal' of every moment.

for them to ever make physical contact; remember the pebble with a quantum wavelength longer than the known universe? This is metaphysics made real. Sets of provisional identicals create eternal time fields at every moment of life for any given individual.

This is a fairly common experience in deep meditation. Spiritual seekers in India and other areas studied this phenomenon for millennia by systematic, focused meditation. Mainstream science can only use highly filtered and limited objective observations. The higher neural functions that take place in minds are currently impossible to analyze. The CIS is, counter intuitively, an ultimately subjective observation that many have seen, but the experience takes extreme discipline and self-training, and cannot be shown to others in conventional ways.

It would be as if scientists wanted to study how top artists create great work; it is currently impossible because it happens in their neural structures. The results would just be a symbolic, massively simplified representation of the neural processes as mathematical data –meaningless outside its real context. This is why spiritual and paranormal activities are considered metaphysics – because of the limitations of current observational technology and scientific models.

The Eternal, Infinite Now

The universe is infinite in matter, energy and extent in all directions. Every moment of your life is happening somewhere in the universe at all times. There is an infinite set of every physically possible moment of life of a sentient being—and, indeed, of all existence. Just like you are the same person you were ten years ago, even though you are made of different molecules, the molecules of the individual bodies of your CIS set are the same by universal pattern equivalence; and so every individual of the set is the same entity.

Limits of the individual physical mind are reduced to insignificance relative to the infinite sets of CISs.

Any limits of the individual physical mind are reduced to insignificance relative to the infinite sets of CISs. Perception and apperception are the neural mechanisms which create eternity from the infinite background of matter and energy. Even an insect unknowingly creates eternal existence for itself since it is a perceiving quantum. This is the ultimate defeat of simple materialism. The sad, boring idea of the lonely individual living and dying once and forever is seen to be a cruel mistake.

The Watcher and the Watched

In science, the concept of an observation is critical and well defined. Merriam-Webster defines observation as "an act of recognizing and noting a fact or occurrence, often involving measurement with instruments," and as "a judgment on or inference from what one has observed."

In mainstream physics, neural systems are considered subjects of outer and inner physical forces, the same as any other mundane object. No special or transcendent mode exists for them in the traditional view. In reality, sentience is infinitely self-contained, self-creating, and self-objective. Even the humblest being has access to the power of infinite reality as a function of its CIS set.

Eternal Consciousness

Through integration of metaset attention, the observation of an object becomes equal to the observation of all its identicals in the. This can be described mathematically as an amplification of a single observation to some particular order of ∞. The identity your mind assigns to the observed object is condensed—waveform 'collapsed', in physics terms—into one superimposed perception by an infinite number of individuals. This is important because it is the mechanism by which a sentience begins to span time and space, creating an

In reality, sentience is infinitely self-contained, self-creating, and self-objective.

experience of reality that transcends individual existence. What we see from the outside as the one-way time flow of a single physical being is in our subjective view, the convergence of an infinite-sentience-set of identical physical individuals at every instant. If personally relative time is slowed sufficiently, this can be observed by the person. This happens as a natural part of life ending: one's life flashes before one's eyes—the 'book of life' is opened.

In the subjective observation of an individual sentience, patterns with high enough similarity can overlap.

In the subjective observation of an individual sentience, patterns with high enough similarity can overlap. This produces a meta-causal mechanism which transcends the traditional physical mechanisms of causality. The death of a physical individual has no more effect on the existence of a consciousness than the splitting of a single water molecule into oxygen and hydrogen has on the existence of water as a pattern category.

Consciously Distinguishable Selves—CDS Set

In some extreme perceptual situations, such as deep meditation, you can experience slightly differing 'versions' of your physical body, its environment, and its history, which are countless light years away. The instantaneous nature of gravity makes obvious an overlap of perceptions between you and these other 'yous'. Indeed, when consciousness is focused in one individual 'you', you in fact perceive that one as yourself. Only upon consciousness shifting into another CDS do you realize its difference from your present consciousness. This corresponds to Cantor's specific infinity set type.

Meditators report this as feeling like awakening several times into slightly different situations. Each awakening is perceived as completely real—and, by UFPI, it may be. This is an extreme perceptual event in which individual consciousness shifts into a different CDS. The overwhelming similarity of the CDS, after the novel feeling of the initial slight difference, shifts the sentience back into 'normal' continuity of consciousness. The realization of each awakening being a different CDS only comes after the next shift, because for that moment that one was you.

Psychology has a name for this—'false awakening'; and, of course, they see it as simply a type of hallucination. But, for those who have lived it and have evidence from their own mind that it is real, it is explained better by fractal ∞. Unlike a simple quantum type like a molecule, though, consciousness in the integrated, infinite form of the CIS has the ability to branch out into any other conscious experience through intergrading of CDSs. A path through tiny variations between individuals of a set is what drives the flow of eternal sentience over the differentiated CDSs. The simultaneous existence of individual sentience patterns and their infinite sets reconciles thorny time/space dualities and the confusions they often cause.

28

Time & Timelessness

Time gives all and takes all away; everything changes,
but nothing perishes

—Giordano Bruno

Duality is not so mysterious: you are an individual who does one thing at a time, yet all the infinite pattern possibilities of your true self are also happening all the time. It is beautiful in its simplicity. Pattern ∞ creates time/eternity periodicity—the dynamic and static Cantorian infinite sets. Regular thinking causes subjective time for a person. Timelessness exists at certain wave nodes of CDS pattern structure—at points of collective perceptual convergence. Wave nodes are points on a vibrating string where vibrations cancel out and there is a still point between the moving parts of the system. A similar effect would logically occur at areas of overlap between subjective experiences of 'Personal Infinity and Eternity'.

Regular thinking causes subjective time for a person.

These fractal nodes of infinite sets, which are time-independent, are not parts of the traditionally defined, objectively observable universe. They are, however, part of the observable universe from the perspective of a CIS. A CIS convergence is timeless because the situation occurs at every relative time in the infinite universe. These convergences are synergistic mind portals for perception of the individual infinite universe—personal eternity. Time-independent nodes within the fractal structure, created by perception, are superposed or imbedded within all time-dependent levels. Duality is once again seen not to be a problem. This mechanism means that all instants of individual consciousness are eternal and inviolable— sacred, to use religious terms.

Since objective reality is described in terms of the mechanisms of waves and particles, think of personal willpower—the primitive drive to stay alive—as the energy that drives the self into 'foreign' realms of consciousness. Emotion—higher apperception of complex energy realities—is the carrier wave that guides this energy, and is formed by the individual structure of each person. This wave guides the CIS on a coherent path among endless potential paths, starting through close CDSs. To perceive the CIS, it seems that emotion must be controlled, spread out over an infinite set and not be taken as an physically individual thing. Meditators experience this as the ability to connect with other consciousnesses. Some religious traditions, like Zen Buddhism, use this technique to make meditation a practical tool to help free other beings from mental strife.

All instants of individual consciousness are eternal and inviolable—sacred, to use religious terms.

Universal Size Relativity and Pattern Similarity negate absolute effects caused by separate fates of CIS set members in space and time. The fractal structure of the infinite universe rules out the death of a consciousness pattern. Time exists for the individual physical mind but not for the individual consciousness, which is an infinite, subjective pattern of near-identical minds.

Only the conscious structure—the person or individual consciousness—who is a part of the set can perceive the infinities of its own sets. Individual consciousness is inviolable and exists eternally. The dualistic paradox of an ∞ of different consciousnesses in the universe is cancelled by the inviolability of the individual. A consciousness can use individual choice to expand or contract its perceptual resolution away from or back to the CIS ego—thus remaining itself or merging into different consciousnesses through CDSs. It always remains individual, though, since a CIS set always exists in every situation.

> **The dualistic paradox of an ∞ of different consciousnesses in the universe is cancelled by the inviolability of the individual.**

Physical "Self"—Eternal Self

When the consciousness of an individual ceases functioning the consciousness appears, to that being, to continue. This is because there is an infinite set of versions of that being, elsewhere, which survived the event that killed the individual member.

This simple scientific implication of the infinite universe brings the old metaphysical idea of the archetype onto solid theoretical terra firma. You, as an individual physical body and nervous system, are not the entirety of your identity. You merely share, temporarily, in the fleeting identity of your current self. Your individual body has a finite life, but your actual self—your archetype, exists eternally.

A CIS set can be seen, in analogy, as a crystal made up of molecules which are similar enough to form a structure which resonates at a certain frequency. A crystal radio worked this way: even though different radios were not in physical contact, they were in meaningful contact by the ability of their circuits to resonate at the same frequency and to be an identical mechanism.

Humans, who share very similar brain structures, letting them understand the same languages, have a similar experience when listening to the messages on that frequency. Obviously, we cannot transmit EM energy to other members of our CIS set, but the metaphor illustrates how pattern equivalence creates a potential connection. Any object of the proper materials and structure can transmit the same message.

Ages and Minds of the Human Being

A common idea in all human cultures is that with age comes wisdom. This is true in the sense that the ego—the everyday symbolic sliver of the mind—of the physical individual, as one goes through the lifecycle, usually becomes more experienced and efficient at navigating everyday life—and better at understanding the physical and social patterns that affect its existence and well-being.

The misconception comes when one begins to believe in a linear progress toward a perfection of oneself based on experience, and that certain stages of life are superior to others. It is traditional to think that an adult in the physical and mental prime of life has a superior grasp on 'reality' than a small child does. Obviously, the adult is in the best condition for evolutionary struggle and success—survival, reproduction and protection of offspring. However, this condition usually comes at a steep price including a significant loss of transcendent insight into their existence in the larger totality of universal experience.

A common idea in all human cultures is that with age comes wisdom.

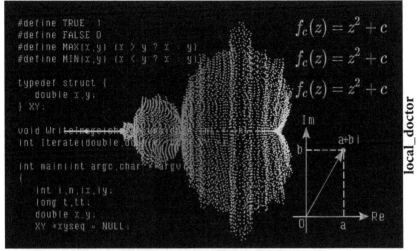

Fractal Brain Equations

The prime adult possesses a much more practical grasp of the immediate individual physical and emotional evolutionary reality, but this is merely one facet of universal reality. Children, in general, are attuned to a significantly larger number of reality 'channels'. Some other states of mind are also more attuned—the very old, some types of mentally ill people, highly artistic people, and so on. These categories of people often need a lot of protection from physical and social dangers. I am not saying that something is wrong with limiting our mental and emotional scope to concentrate on evolutionary imperatives. That is just how the human lifecycle works. There is obviously a time in individual life when that is necessary for continuation of humanity. This is how the biological mechanism works, to put it bluntly, but there are other mechanisms of consciousness that crystallize from this.

Kids think with a certain brand of simple common sense which is all too often dismissed as naivety as we get older. They are a lot closer to the pure reality of the non-symbolic mind, which is usually only weakened as we grow older. This weakening closes a lot of doors to alternative ways of approaching a question. Younger minds are not distracted by the symbolic junk and the social, emotional and financial considerations that adults often are. These distractions obscure our inborn abilities to have insight into the universe with our own non-symbolic minds.

Hindu philosophy recognizes this and has institutionalized the practice of elderly people embarking on personal meditative journeys back to the insights of universal reality. After their time of focusing on individual earthly responsibilities, they rediscover the realms of infinite being that had been put on hold. For elderly people, evolutionary pressures coming from lower brain areas have been worked out during life to the point that the higher brain functions can once more be developed and enjoyed. Many serious problems in society can be traced back to the discounting of the specialized insights of different stages of life and the exclusive lionization of the prime evolutionary stage.

29

Eternal Life & Infinite Consciousness

We have seen that death is an illusion but, during what we could call the ultimate CIS experience, we consciously put together our lives and everything we learned at all stages. Other people, who died young in our objective version, lived on to ripe old age through the 'subjective' experience of the totality of their CIS sets. Many people report their 'lives flashing before their eyes' after near-death experiences.

The closer and closer approach to absolute states and particles is a goal in physics. The Big Bang and the 'heat death' of the universe are examples of ideas of absolutes coming from the questionable idea of the universe being finite. These forced absolutes ignore both true time relativity springing from size relativity, and infinite fractal periodicity of being. They also deny the wonderful possibility of personally experiencing eternity, which we can do, by using the higher-order perceptual mechanisms

Belief in an absolute beginning and end of the universe and its subsystems, including human consciousness, is not necessary and not supported by philosophy and science.

evolved into our nervous systems. Belief in an absolute beginning and end of the universe and its subsystems, including human consciousness, is not necessary and is not supported by philosophy and science.

The Shared Universal Consciousness

A big question some will have is, what if one wants it to end? My best hypothesis is that ego mind ends by choice; and many spiritual thinkers through history have thought the same. Mortality can be transcended when the collective consciousness of the CIS set knows that it is dying, then perceives its own eternity, as well as the eternity of all possible life experiences of the individual. It then voluntarily separates itself from the infinite sets of physical bodies that generated it.

Belief in an absolute beginning and end of the universe and its subsystems, including human consciousness, is not necessary and is not supported by philosophy and science.

Where does it go? Maybe it works its way out into the entirety of its life CIS sets in a ripple effect –through memories (much of what we call memories may actually be sentient connections to other selves concurrently in existence during other relative 'time' stages of our lives). Those with unpleasant lives can take comfort in knowing that, like the rest of us, all the perfection of the universe is united within you; and the pain of your personal experiences is shared among all others, as is the joy, peace and wonder of all others shared with you.

Memory shows strong indications of being a non-local quantum effect. A real-time connection to all times of life allows all individuals of a set see that consciousness is infinite: all times of life still exist in the present. When

all individuals of a set lock **An infinite set of eter-**
into place in this ultimate **nally sentient individuals**
realization, self-release is **chooses, in unison, to**
possible. An infinite set of **end its individuality and**
eternally sentient individuals **strike out into the wider**
chooses, in unison, to end **world of consciousness.**
its individuality and strike out into the wider world of
consciousness.

The individual CIS/CDS consciousness can cascade out into other consciousnesses connected to its own throughout its life path. Final resolution of the ultimate question for an individual is achieved by the focus of collective perceptual mechanisms toward ∞. This is done using the matrix of an infinite set of identical and nearly-identical selves. Absolute assurance of final peace of mind allows the individual physical sentience to let go of their finite, illusory limitations. They are secure in the knowledge that all life is eternal and ultimately one being, and they can now be fully part of it once again. People who become proficient at advanced meditation or sleep control can observe the moment when perfect balance between the conscious and subconscious minds occurs. They often become familiar with the connection of different physical minds.

Infinite Deaths, Infinite Lives

Remember, in an infinite universe, there are always infinite sets of 'you' that are dying, so the process of actualization of eternal and infinite life for you goes on constantly and endlessly; it is happening right now. There is nothing scary or weird or unfamiliar about it. Many people can remember these realities from early childhood, and they feel familiar and comfortable. In most people, they become overwritten by social conditioning and trivial memories.

However, the individual consciousness reconnects with the feeling during death, as a result of 'seeing'—and then becoming—the entirety of the eternal CIS –the True Self of spiritual tradition. It is simply a letting go of our focus on a system of temporary brain circuits –the everyday ego. The True Self then appears a perfectly stable quantum to others that can be interacted with to form higher transcendent structural realities.

Ancient Mind Philosophy

In general, when a physical individual dies, that individual consciousness itself likely perceives a close call—and then life goes on because the consciousness pattern still exists in an infinite set of CIS individuals who survived the event. If an individual consciousness is focused on the CIS where he or she is very old and dying, at some point, because of physical limitations, these subjective, near-death experiences recur occur more and more quickly until a saturation point is reached. At that point the individual consciousness merges with the infinite CIS/CDS set. They all begin to 'feel' each other; the insulation of the individual ego is removed by identical perceptual death events approaching ∞.

So, when a physical individual dies, it is objectively a matter of an isolated physical system ceasing to function; but when a consciousness 'dies' it is subjectively the perceptual event of an ever-accelerating number of physical deaths approaching ∞—remember the relativity of infinities. There is always a Consciously Selectable infinite CIS set component of the consciousness that does not physically die in any given situation. By Cantor's principle of differential infinities, however, the relative importance, to an individual consciousness, of survivor CIS experiences drops off exponentially as the individual ages or is injured so seriously that physical survival is not realistic. This accelerating and seemingly endless death/renewal perception overwhelms the individual ego perception. Eventually, the resistance—that the individual consciousness and its associated situational CIS set had—to merging with the infinite, overarching set of all CIS/CDSs is overcome.

In the first case, the individual realizes that the rebirth cycle trend is going toward an infinitely old individual. This is seen to be illogical and undesirable. When the cycle accelerates to a speed beyond the perceptual tolerance of the individual, all the infinite deaths and rebirths blur into one. The consciousness tends to choose the path of infinite non-ego instead. We see that our individual experience is perceived as critical for us from the view of other people, because they are not parts of our CIS. For an infinite consciousness set, physically individual experiences are not critical. Death,

Death, which is merely cessation of local sentient experience, is falsely seen as an eternal loss of existence.

which is merely cessation of local sentient experience, is falsely seen as an eternal loss of existence. This mainstream idea about death is, of course, a tragic illusion.

In the case of unsurvivable injuries, this natural pattern ∞ phenomenon acting from the nervous system also takes place. This, like the previous example, is a case of the experience of becoming an infinitely limited physical individual. The person runs into the limit of the ∞ of their set, so why not break through it? Imagine a person is so badly injured that there is no possibility that they will live, from the point of view of an outside observer. The person is seen as dying by other people, but, through their own field of consciousness, that person experiences survival by pattern similarity of a very closely related CDS where the injury is slightly less severe, which causes the person to live a little longer. These perceptible spans may eventually get down to milliseconds or less. In Tibetan yoga philosophy, these are known as bardo states, phases of entry into the 'afterlife'. These are extreme perceptual breaks in our sense of individuality, leading to a realization of oneness with other minds.

In Tibetan yoga philosophy, these are known as bardo states, phases of entry into the 'afterlife'.

30

The "Mortal Coil" & Impermanence

In much popular religious philosophy, though, the impermanence of the individual state of mind is emphasized, almost fetishized. This is unfortunate because it is scientifically false—remember the illusion of the wave/particle duality. Every instant of our lives exists forever. The scope of our possible experiences and states of mind rests upon the entirety of the physical realities we went through as a physical individual, but which still exist. Our individual CIS mind becomes multi-modal during the death experience. We can multitask, spiritually, beyond individual physical time and revisit various stages of life to work from them at a meta-individual level.

This scientific view is reflected in the Buddhist concepts of dharma—working our way through life as an ego personality with an eye on the effects in the afterlife—and karma—the mental and moral situations we as conscious nervous systems must experience as a result of our genetics—the effects of our own and our ancestors' actions on our lives as well as those of other

This scientific view is reflected in the Buddhist concepts of dharma—and karma.

people and places we have encountered. This 'mortal coil' of a person is the basis of eternal life and must be worked out and linked to its non-ego, non-symbolic mirror of perfected being.

Although we will not know until it happens to us, when the time of death of the physical individual begins we may feel a break in continuity and experience a pattern-similarity-mediated perceptual shift to a closely situated CDS—beginning at the point that its slightly longer lifespan begins. In its turn, the sentience of this CDS meta-individual shifts to another CDS set which is situated to die physically a tiny bit later than the second CDS set. This process can continue ad infinitum since the possibility is open that a chain of CDS sets can be continually perceived in which death is forestalled sequentially, for example by 0.5, 0.25, 0.125, 0.0625 microseconds, and so on.

I Become, Therefore I Am

This chain of perception either shifts toward ∞ in the direction of timelessness as an infinitely limited individual, or it moves to a CDS range where the members survive the injury and thus creates a near-death experience. The experience of timelessness in the first case may enable the individual consciousness to merge with the absolute ∞ of consciousness. This is a function of infinite matter and energy configured into all physically possible pattern sets

> The experience of timelessness in the first case may enable the individual consciousness to merge with the absolute ∞ of consciousness.

which exists forever and everywhere; but it is only realized individually at the point of cessation of individual infinite set consciousness. It creates infinite higher-order time, space and consciousness effects, beyond the possibility of human understanding. While growing into this, a consciousness cherry picks the best of the best of it to be part of and share with others.

The Meta-Self and Physical Immortality

Individuals step out of dying meta-self like we would step out of a theatre showing a boring film. The meta-self is recognized as a temporary image –one among an infinite range of choices. This is not a scary loss or grounds for a sappy, bittersweet religious saying. We do something like this every day when we decide to shift our conscious attention away from what we judge unimportant or unpleasant to us and focus it on something more worthy. We laugh after a terror-inspiring situation when we see that we are okay. We get interested in some new facet of reality when the usual becomes boring. Safe in the knowledge that we and all our loved ones exist together forever, our personal business concluded, we each move on to bigger and better things.

With our technology, we may sooner or later have the ability to transfer the consciousness produced by a brain into a computer, and that will still be a physical individual. The computer-based consciousness will eventually go through the same CIS/CDS 'death' process as it ages or is neglected or destroyed by those responsible for its maintenance. The same principles apply no matter what medium carries the consciousness as long as it is a system which can recognize its own pattern, and simultaneously is that pattern. Given enough time, all isolated, physically individual systems decline and cease to exist.

Us and Them in ∞

CIS and CDS sets must be, in turn, connected to higher order infinite consciousness sets in a similar manner— by the principle of universal fractal pattern ∞. The dualistic paradox of an ∞ of different consciousnesses in the universe is reconciled with the inviolability of the individual by the principle of individual choice. A consciousness can voluntarily limit its perceptual resolution to the CIS ego or expand it. It chooses to remain itself or to merge with different consciousnesses through a fractal ladder of infinite gradations into the micro and macro realms of emergent properties of matter. It always remains individual, though, since its discrete infinite sets always exist and can always be returned to.

The commonly observed phenomena of a person's life 'flashing before their eyes', 'perfect recall', time appearing to slow down or stand still, and the instinctual idea of the 'Infinite Return' may all be—among many other mystical and oft-dismissed phenomena—perceptual artifacts of CIS mechanisms. More extreme effects, such as the feeling of past lives and reincarnation, are also indications related to this.

Your and my existence are time-dependent and limited from the viewpoint of other people, but are subjectively time-independent and unlimited. From the perception of other people, our lives are finite and we have evolved to see ourselves in that way –we need to see ourselves as others do to survive as individuals. But this is ultimately incorrect. It was an evolutionarily necessary condition dating back to the evolution of simple animals— **There are common** competitive survival, reproduction, **denominators within** and care of the young. We are still **matter and energy** animals, of course, but a type which **that make unity with** was described by William Blake — **all physical exis-** halfway between apes and angels. **tence the objective,**

There are common denominators **natural state of our** within matter and energy that make **nervous systems.** unity with all physical existence the objective, natural state of our nervous systems. The next arena of human evolution is in the subjective study and practice of the eternity of the true self and its infinite connections to all other consciousnesses. Infinite matter and energy —> Pattern as expressed in Quanta and Qualia —> Pattern ∞ in the form of Fractal behavior —> Pattern Eternity--created by time perception of a sentience in an infinite, fractally-structured environment—> Superfinite consciousness.

31

Conclusions

*…This is the most enormous extension of vision of which
life is capable: the projection of itself into other lives. This
is the lonely, magnificent power of humanity. It is far
more than any spatial adventure, the supreme epitome
of reaching out.*

—Loren Eisley
The Immense Journey

The idea of the physical mind being a material pattern recognition mechanism, no matter how complex, is unacceptable to many people. This comes from a feeling that our true nature is beyond the physical realm. There is truth in this feeling, but scientific knowledge of pattern complexity can help on the path to understanding the eternal nature of both individual and collective consciousness. When we begin to really understand that

We a feeling that our true nature is beyond the physical realm.

what has always been called divinity comes from a physical ability to sense the infinite and convert it into the eternal, we set ourselves on the road to the rational, timeless quest for our true selves and our connection and reconciliation with all others. With further philosophical refinement and scientific research, this will become more and more a function of the ultimate discoveries of human potential.

By understanding and experiencing infinite universal pattern equivalence, we can transcend physical barriers to understanding the universe. We do not have to put ourselves through intellectual contortions trying to explain the strange monsters that lie beyond the reach of our telescopes and microscopes. We do not have to assume that only experts in particle physics and astrophysics can have ideas on what the universe is and how it works. The universe is here with us on all levels. Chaos science and universal fractal geometry show us that no pattern category is more real or absolute than any other.

The Illusion of Finitude

This is the basic essence of Copernican thinking, and the logically unavoidable principle of infinitely repeating fractal size relativity, in both size directions, provides a mechanism of infinite and eternal existence. This is difficult to accept because it clashes with the default—evolutionarily stableperceptual regime of humankind, which limits itself to finite thinking as a practical mechanism. The illusory finitude presented to us by our own minds is usually taken as a first principle indicating universal finitude. Because we appear to be mortal, it is thought that the universe must be mortal. This is not legitimate reasoning; it is presuming the default perceptual mode of our primitive brain mechanisms to be a central axiom of the entirety of existence.

> The illusory finitude presented to us by our own minds is usually taken as a first principle indicating universal finitude.

The individual ego holds its temporal existence symbolically outside of the size relative fractal pattern ∞. This is an effect of evolutionary requirements, of brain evolution, to favor self-preservation instincts. You cannot struggle effectively for survival if your mind is too often in a state of realization that its existence is independent of any single individual physical body. An organism would tend to lower its guard and not put as much effort into reproduction and care of the young. As humans, we are at the evolutionary stage of being able to know and use this reality to improve and enrich ourselves.

Our Personal Cosmos

Our cosmos is everything you have ever perceived, all the present and future potentials for perception, and all the infinite experience of your CIS sets. Free will combined with unique experiences and emotions are parts of the 'carrier wave' that the individual uses to make their experiential and perceptual path through the universe.

Do not let anyone tell you that science says you are 'just atoms' and that all that exists is just atoms bouncing around from the movement of energy waves. The scientific facts are that your body is entirely made of atoms and all that exists does consist of atoms and energy, but this language ignores emergent properties and infinite potential for complexity. It also disregards the creation of meaning by conscious mechanisms. The word 'just' is the problem. This type of reductionist interpretation is a belittlement of reality. It is an unnecessarily empty, and ultimately futile, attempt to make reality manageable for the symbolic mind in its current embodiment. It wrongly takes the transcendent power out of science.

Many scientists think there are contradictions between finite/infinite and time/timelessness because they think everything must be, eventually, proven experimentally. If it is not currently possible to support something experimentally, it is often considered to be metaphysics, or else it is simply ignored. Our ancestors, for thousands of years, knew that there are real things that we can know outside of the limitations imposed by our physical senses and the modern scientific method. They had much more respect for what we call intuition.

Many scientists think there are contradictions between finite/infinite and time/timelessness.

Taking Transcendence Seriously

We need, once again, to start taking this seriously so we can make further strides in understanding ourselves and the universe—which are much closer to one another than we think. We often read things in popular science publications like, 'our relation to the universe', but this type of thinking separates us into a category away from everything else. It is almost as strange and simple as thinking that the universe is only the stuff we see in the night sky outside of the earth's atmosphere, or that the sun revolves around the earth.

Philosopher Ernst Cassirer says of the legacy of Giordano Bruno:

Man no longer lives in the world of a prisoner enclosed within the narrow walls of a finite, physical universe. The infinite universe sets no limits to human reason; on the contrary, it is the great incentive of human reason. The human intellect becomes aware of its own infinity through measuring its own powers by the infinite universe.

Indeed, the intuitive, the transcendental, is once again being brought back into science by avant-garde quantum physicists, chaos scientists and others. The epic universal vision of Bruno and many others, in which the merging of dualities of the mystical/rational, scientific/spiritual, essence/symbol are reconciled, is coming back to restore the balance that has long been tipped too far to the style of science, which is experimental, linear, utilitarian, and lucrative.

Think of everyone you know and yourself as infinite sets taking yourselves, mistakenly, as finite entities.

Sadness, fear for lost loved ones, and loneliness from being an isolated physical individual are natural; but instead try think of everyone you know and yourself as infinite sets taking yourselves, mistakenly, as finite entities. You are, briefly, suffering from an illusion caused by localized physical limitations within an infinite existence. If life becomes miserable for you or others, and if the situation seems unbearable, remember that any single experience in life is eternal and can be used as a starting point into larger eternal sets. So, there is a way back to happier, more promising times.

> "The most precious of flowers once bloomed, consumed by the fires of time and avarice."
> —William Leonard Pickard,
> **The Rose of Paracelsus**

References & Further Reading

Alexander, Amir. *Infinitesimal: How a Dangerous Mathematical Theory Shaped the Modern World*. New York, 2014.

Bagaria, Joan. Set Theory, *The Stanford Encpedia of Philosophy* (Winter 2017 Edition), Edward N. Zalta (ed.), https://plato.stanford.edu/archives/win2017/entries/set-theory/

Berrill, N.J. *You and the Universe*. Fawcett Publications Inc, Greenwich, CT, 1959.

Bohm, David. *Wholeness and the Implicate Order*. New York, Routledge Classics, 1980.

Borges, Jorge Luis. *Labyrinths*. New Directions Publishing Corporation. New York, 1964.

Calvino, Italo. *Cosmicomics*. The Macmillan Company. New York, 1965.

Cantor, Georg. *Contributions to the Founding of the Theory of Transfinite Numbers,* (1915), Dover Books, 1955..

Cantor's Infinity: Taking the Next Step. https://mathworld.wolfram.com/CantorSet.html

Cassirer, Ernst. *Essay on Man: Introduction to the Philosophy of Human Culture*. Berlin, Yale University Press, 1944.

Deutsch, David. *The Fabric of Reality: The Science of Parallel Universes--and Its Implications*. New York, Penguin Books, 1998.

Einstein, Albert. *Relativity: The Special and General Theory*, Princeton University Press, 2018

Eisely,Loren. *The Immense Journey*. New York, Vintage Books, 1959.

Gamow, George. *One Two Three... Infinity: Facts and Speculations of Science*. New York, Dover Pub., 1988.

Gleick, James. *Chaos, Making A New Science*. Viking Penguin Inc. New York, 1987.

Heller, Michael, Lemaitre, Georges. *Big Bang and the Quantum Universe:* With His Original Manuscript (History of Astronomy Series. 1996.

Hoyle, Fred. *The Intelligent Universe*. Holt, Rinehart & WInton, 1988.

Jung, Carl. *The Archetypes and The Collective Unconscious*. London, Routledger, 1996.

Kant, Immanuel. Critique of Pure Reason. 1781.

Leary, Timothy. *Musings on Human Metamorphoses*. Ronin Publishing, 2003.

Leslie, John. *Infinite Minds*. Oxford University Press, 2001.

Lucretius. *On the Nature of Things*. Washington Square Press Inc. New York, 1965.

Mishra, Rammurti. *Fundamentals of Yoga*. New York, Julian Press, 1959.

Nietzsche, Friedrich. *The Joyful Wisdom*. Chemnitz. 1882.

Oparin, A.I. *The Origin of Life*. The Macmillan Company. New York, 1938.

Penrose, Roger. Fashion, *Faith, and Fantasy in the New Physics of the Universe*. Princeton University Press, 2016.

Reader, John. *The Rise of Life: The First 3.5 Billion Years. Sources and Studies of History of Mathematics*, New York, 1986 and Physical Science. 2004

Wallis, John. *The Arithmetic of Infinitesimals: Sources and Studies in the History of Mathematics and Physical Sciences,* (1656) Springer-Verlag.

White, Michael. *The Pope & The Heretic. The Story of Giordano Bruno, The Man Who Dared to Defy the Soman Inquisition.* HarperCollins, New York, 2002.

Wittgenstein, Josef. *Tractatus Logico-Philosophicus.*

Author Bio

Michael Townsand is a biologist/chemist with a great interest in the history and philosophy of science and cosmology. Mr. Townsand invites comments, questions, and critiques at townsandmg@gmail.com.

RONIN Books
for Independent Minds

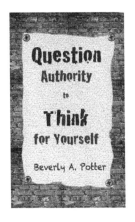

Visit Ronin's site *www.roninpub.com* to see these and other of Ronin books. Use isbn to order from any bookstore. ENJOY!

CPSIA information can be obtained
at www.ICGtesting.com
Printed in the USA
JSHW022249170321
12620JS00008B/394